SPC for Short Run Manufacturing

By
Leonard A. Doty

Hanser Gardner Publications
Cincinnati

Leonard A. Doty

Includes bibliographical references and index.
ISBN 1-56990-239-9
1. Process control--Statistical methods. 2. Quality control--Statistical methods. I. Title.
TS156.8.D67 1997
658.5'65--dc21 97-35838
CIP

While the advice and information in *SPC for Short Run Manufacturing* are believed to be true, accurate and reliable, neither the author or the publisher can accept any legal responsibility for any errors, omissions, or damages that may arise out of the use of this information. The author and publisher make no warranty of any kind, expressed or implied, with regard to the material contained in this work.

Hanser Gardner Publications
6915 Valley Avenue
Cincinnati, OH 45244-3029

TABLE OF CONTENTS

PREFACE

This book presents the fundamental theory, practices, and procedures of Statistical Process Control (SPC) for a small manufacturing firm. Throughout, every effort has been made to tailor the book to the particular needs of small manufacturers, and the examples and text are intended to address their needs. Since the control of quality is a basic management function, and SPC provides the most precise, and in the long run the least costly, method for that control, it is hoped that this book will provide the tools needed by smaller firms to be competitive in the marketplace.

To provide the reader with the perspective to understand how and why quality has gained significance in all fields of industry, the book opens with an outline of SPC and then gives a general description and history of quality. Chapter 2 introduces the theory behind control charts and Chapter 3 is essential for understanding the normal curve (the normal curve forms the basis from which all SPC control charts are constructed). This presentation leads naturally into the discussion of control charts in Chapters 4 through 6. In these chapters the topics covered include rules for constructing and using control charts; how to apply necessary variables and attributes charts; and how control charts are analyzed to reduce variation and to improve quality. In Chapter 7, methods of analysis other than control charts are presented. Finally, Chapter 8 has a discussion on standard sampling plans and shows how they are constructed and analyzed, presents the most used standard sampling plan (MIL-STD-105E), and shows how it is used. Some aspects and difficulties inherent in the nonproduction portion of a manufacturing plant are presented in the section on "Nonmanufacturing SPC" in Chapter 7 and in the section on "Employee Evaluation" in Chapter 6.

I am indebted to many colleagues for their encouragement and assistance; especially the Tucson chapter of the American Society for Quality Control (ASQC), Dr. Michael Leeming, and Luis Soto. As always, I am especially indebted to my wife, Lucy, without whose help and encouragement this book could not have been written.

— Chapter 1 —

SPC AND QUALITY

There are probably only two overall management systems: "bottom line" or profit-driven systems where the focus is always on money, and customer-driven systems where the focus is on people.

People (especially managers) in a profit-driven system tend to concentrate on people control (the dominance, manipulation, and influence of people), blame, recrimination, production and accounting (things and money), autocratic management, and the "bottom line" (profit, return on investment, etc.). In these systems, reports and paperwork tend to become more important than people and their reactions; people tend to be treated as if they are only units of production; and customers tend to be viewed as only a necessary evil (with such things as massive advertisements and various inducements being used to hold customers instead of making quality products and treating customers properly).

On the other hand, people in a customer-driven system have a completely different corporate philosophy and attitude, which then requires completely different types of procedures. Quality and customer satisfaction are integral to this system, and management and workers cooperate to solve problems, build quality, and satisfy customers' expectations. Employees as well as customers are treated with respect and courtesy, and supportive rather than autocratic management procedures are used. Cooperation is extremely important in a customer-driven system (it has been found that cooperation *almost always* results in better performance; while cooperation plus training *always* results in better performance — usually much better).

Of course, profits are important in a customer-driven system and customers are important in a "bottom line" system. It is the focus that matters. In a profit-driven system the focus is on material objects and money, even though customers are present and things must be done to keep them. But in a customer-driven system, even though the production of products and the saving of money are important, the focus is on people (customers, employees, etc.), and procedures are organized to make them happy and satisfied. Also, a customer-driven system emphasizes the long-term health and longevity of the firm while a profit-driven system tends to be more concerned with short-term profits and the quarterly report. Although a customer-driven system focuses on the customer and on quality rather than profits, it has been found that a quality concentration eventually leads to higher profits, although the profits tend to come somewhat more slowly (instead of at the next quarterly report).

This new system (focusing on customers and people rather than things and money) has been given many names, but the term TQM (Total Quality Management) is most often used, and is the term that will be used throughout this book. However, the technical arm of TQM is SPC (Statistical Process Control), and SPC is what this book is all about. Since the central concept of SPC is quality, this chapter explains the main quality functions. But first, some important aspects of the nature of SPC are explained (in order to give the reader a good idea, right at the start, of what SPC is all about).

THE NATURE OF SPC

Besides being the technical arm of TQM, SPC can also be a system itself. In either case, the important SPC elements are as follows:

1. QUALITY. This is, of course, the main thrust of SPC. After all, SPC is a technique that assists in the increase of quality. Therefore, it is important that the main quality functions be understood. These functions are explained in the remaining sections of this chapter.
2. CONTROL CHARTS. Control charts cannot solve problems, only people can do this. What control charts do is to provide information that can be used to identify problem causes and suggest possible solutions (also, control charts often identify problems where none was known to exist before). Chapters 4, 5, and 6 explain the use of control charts.
3. ANALYSIS OF INFORMATION. This means to examine information to see if it can lead to the identification of problems, causes, and possible solutions. Control charts are the single most used method in SPC to accomplish this (see Chapter 6). However, there are others (see Chapter 7).

4. ACCEPTANCE SAMPLING. This refers to the inspection of purchased goods and services (see Chapter 8). It is an important function of Receiving — so important that it is often accomplished in a department by itself, called Receiving Inspection. There are some people who think that SPC will supplant acceptance sampling because supplier companies will all have SPC, making Acceptance Sampling redundant. Even if this occurs (and that seems doubtful), it will take a long time to accomplish. Actually, it seems as if there will always be some need for acceptance sampling.
5. IMPROVEMENT. This is also called Constant Improvement (CI), Profit Improvement (PI), Quality Improvement (QI), etc. There are two ways to do this. One is to correct the process problems, and the other is to change the process parameters. In Chapter 6 there is a more complete discussion of these two very important concepts.
6. VARIATION REDUCTION. This means to make the product so that the measurements, or observations, are as close to the center of the specifications as possible (if all product measurements were exactly at the process center, there would be no variation). As this occurs, the standard deviation gets smaller (see Chapters 2 and 6).
7. PROCESS VERSUS PRODUCT. Control charts are concerned only with the process. A perfect process, it is assumed, makes perfect products. It is also true that the product must be compared to the process (after the process has been perfected). This is done by Engineering, to determine if the process can produce the product as designed; and by Production, to see if the process can be improved so that a better product can be made (see Chapter 6).
8. COST. The purpose here is to make the product at the lowest possible cost. It is probably best to think of costs as occurring in two ways — as quality costs and as production costs (actually, these are just two ways of thinking about, and analyzing, costs). In general, quality improvement activities tend to reduce production costs, while quality costs are usually reduced by balancing failure costs with prevention and appraisal costs (see "The Cost of Quality" section later in this chapter).
9. PRODUCTIVITY. This refers to the maximization of production and the minimization of costs. The purpose here is to make, and ship, as much product as possible at the lowest cost possible. However, if the focus is on producing as many products as possible regardless of problems or any other factor (as is often the case in profit-motivated systems), quality is usually damaged and productivity is seldom increased. On the other hand, customer-driven systems are constantly improving quality (this is one of their most important imperatives),

which in turn always includes increased productivity as well (if only in the reduction of scrap and rework).

10. STATISTICS. Increases in quality can occur without statistics, and Chapter 7 gives several procedures where this is possible. However, SPC cannot really exist without statistics, especially with control charts (see Chapters 2 – 6). In fact, control charts without statistics are impossible.
11. CONTROLS. SPC is very data oriented and monitors thousands of variations, inside and outside the organization. These numerical measurements are used to guide the search for answers to problems and to find better ways of doing things. They are not used to control people. People have the freedom to use these data-based controls to bring about improvements.
12. AN ORIENTATION TOWARD PREVENTION rather than correction. In SPC, the overriding attitude is to keep errors from happening. This is done in two ways. First, when errors do occur, SPC provides information that assists in reorganizing the system so that these errors are not repeated. Second, many charts (especially variables charts) provide information to correct problems before errors happen. Therefore, in a good SPC system, errors will be kept to a minimum, rather than just letting them occur and then constantly correcting them afterwards.
13. DOE (Design of Experiments). This is a highly statistical and highly quantitative procedure used for identifying those process parameters that are causing problems (see Montgomery, 1991; also see Doty, 1996, Chapter 10 for a short summary of DOE). DOE takes a whole book to properly explain. Some think that DOE is a separate system and should not be included with SPC. DOE is not covered in this book.
14. DOCUMENTS, PROCEDURES, AND RECORDS. A document is a written description of something, such as a sales order, a purchase agreement, a list of what is to be done or what has been accomplished, etc. A procedure is a description, or list, of what must be done. Although a procedure does not have to be written, it should be (procedures are often grouped together in a book called the Book of Quality Procedures, and summarized as QP's). A record is a documented written description of something that has been accomplished. It is often required, by customers, to provide a means for backtracking and analyzing when a problem occurs (called an "audit trail"). Most, if not all, of the following list of procedures and records would probably be needed by a complete quality system. The SPC practitioner should check this list to see just which of these pro-

cedures are necessary (others, not listed here, may be needed for various specific requirements).

- A management policy statement.
- Organizational charts.
- Management review plans and quality audit reports.
- Contract review plans.
- Design/development plans.
- Plans for the handling of documents, including a master list with the current revisions of all documents.
- A list of approved vendors, and a description of how they are approved.
- Production/quality plans, or work orders.
- Equipment manuals.
- Process procedures.
- Work instructions.
- Workmanship standards.
- The identification, documentation, evaluation, segregation, and disposition of all nonconforming material.
- Procedures for investigating causes for nonconforming conditions and initiating corrective actions, as well as records of these actions.
- Procedures for identification, collection, indexing, filing, storage, maintenance, and disposition of quality records.
- Employee certification and training plans and records.
- Statistical techniques.
- Product identification records.
- Inspection and testing records.
- Calibration records.

15. HUMANISTIC. These are the people interactions that are not technical in nature. Actually they are more TQM than SPC, but people often think of them as belonging to SPC, and tend to include them in an SPC program. Probably the biggest differences between the people interactions in SPC and those in TQM are the formality that accompanies them, and the attitudes of the people involved and of those in charge. In SPC, these humanistic aspects tend to be quite casual and unofficial, with people being aware of and using them on an individual basis. With TQM, however, formal rules and programs, with one or more facilitators, are instituted for each of these aspects (at least those that apply to the firm concerned), and everyone is trained and helped to use them. The most important of these humanistic aspects are listed below. For more on this subject, see: Covey, 1989; Deming, 1986; Peters, 1987 (especially his Chapter 1); Schatz, 1986;

Scholtes, 1988; Scott and Jaffe, 1991; and "The Total Quality Management Guide" from the Department of Defense.

a. Teams, of those involved, are formed to solve problems. This is called the "team approach to problem solving," and in TQM the teams are rather permanent with facilitators to train and assist. In SPC, however, these teams tend to be transitory and less formal, and are normally formed to solve a single problem and then disbanded.
b. Workers are given some of the authority that used to be reserved solely for managers. They become more responsible for their work and for quality, do their own measurements, and make their own changes for improvement. Sometimes they even do some of the planning, at least as far as their own work is concerned.
c. A climate of respect, courtesy, and appreciation is fostered. People are treated with dignity and respect and, therefore, tend to work together more harmoniously and to have more feelings of belonging — i.e., of being a part of an organization. Rewards go beyond simple benefits and salary to the belief that "we are a family; we do good work."
d. Everyone feels strongly about the customer and tends to feel more personally responsible for customer satisfaction and for delivering quality to the customer. A caring attitude is fostered, and everyone works together for the good of the company and does whatever is needed to enhance the customer's image of the company — the image of how well the company does on quality, and how well it treats the customer.
e. A customer/supplier attitude is more prevalent in the firm (you are the customer of the last person to work on the product, and the supplier to the next).
f. Supervisors use supportive styles, instead of being autocratic bosses, and work together with the workers to effect improvements. People are allowed, actually encouraged, to participate in problem solving. This is in marked contrast to former times when the workers were almost completely excluded from any discussions and any decisions about improvements or changes.
g. The attitude of blame and recrimination of the past is replaced with an attitude of fixing the problem instead of fixing the blame. It has been found that most problems (95% according to Dr. W. Edwards Deming, and according to most Japanese quality experts) are systems oriented anyway, so that individuals, although involved, are not the real cause of problems (occasionally they are,

of course, but not often). It's the system that must be blamed, and then changed, and only managers can change the system. This leaves the workers with an enormous feeling of relief, since they now do not have to be ever mindful of being held accountable for something over which they have no real control (they no longer feel that they have to spend much of their time and energy on protecting themselves). Once again, this is an informal feeling that tends to develop in SPC systems. In TQM, however, formal procedures are instituted to assure that these kind of feelings, and these kind of actions, really do occur.

h. Because of these things, everyone tends to be happier at his or her job.

IMPLEMENTING SPC

SPC implementation procedures should be kept as simple as possible although that is sometimes difficult to do; complex interacting process variables may sometimes require more complex implementation procedures (for example, complex mathematical models may be needed at any of the steps for identification and/or analysis of the important factors). Remember that SPC tends to use a few simple things in a nonformal way. When too many things, along with too much formality, are used, the resultant system tends to become TQM rather than SPC (which can be a very good thing — SPC should be used as a stepping stone to TQM). The list below is a simple summary of the important SPC implementation steps, and is provided to present an overall picture to the analysts involved.

These implementation steps are not static (that is, each always following in the same order) but are dynamic procedures that require constant attention, as well as the flexibility to adapt to any and all special problems as they are discovered. At any one step, information found there can suggest improvements and refinements to the system so that backtracking, repeating, and/or resequencing of steps tend to be commonplace.

1. Assign a special facilitator (usually the top quality manager) to the SPC program, and train that person in SPC. It is also possible to use a team of top managers (with at least one worker, and one or more facilitators) instead of an individual. A team, however, is more of a TQM, rather than an SPC, approach. In any case, a team is almost always best.
2. Develop flow charts for all products (see the section entitled "Flow Charts" in Chapter 7). Make sure that all quality measurement spots are considered (these are usually places where inspections are needed) and shown on the flow charts.

3. Identify critical operations. Ask operators, engineers, etc. Do Pareto analyses, cause and effect analyses, etc. (see Chapter 7). Analyze defect rates, costs, etc. List these operations in order of criticality and by cost, defect rate, percent defective, product, operation importance, etc.
4. Choose a problem (often a spot on the production line) that should be easily corrected, and will be most likely to result in a large cost improvement. An obvious choice would be an operation with a large cost — a large cost improvement cannot be effected without a large cost already occurring. In this way, the rest of the firm can see that SPC really works — that it actually produces cost cutting procedures.
5. Install a chart at the problem area, collect the data, and plot the chart (see Chapters 4 and 5).
6. Analyze the chart(s) as enough data become available (see Chapter 6). Correct assignable causes and make process improvements as suggested by chart data and chart interpretation.
7. Using the improvement shown by this first control chart success, sell the project to others and get their cooperation. This is a very important step. Without the full cooperation of others (management included), SPC will not succeed.
8. After the first process has been changed, and after improvement using SPC has been proved, gradually install control charts in all other areas — following the steps listed above. Team type brainstorming can, and almost always should, be used at every step along the way. Also, any (and sometimes all) of the analysis tools of Chapter 7 can be used at any of these steps.
9. Construct quality plans for each product and each chart (who and how inspect, how much, how often, what tools, when inspect, etc.).
10. Install control charts in service areas, and areas other than production, as needed.
11. Install a cost control system to control quality costs (see the section in this chapter entitled "Quality Costs").
12. As circumstances permit, use some of the people, or humanistic, aspects of TQM (as has been explained in the last section). In SPC, of course, these things usually tend to be somewhat casual and unofficial. If they do become a formal aspect of the management system, they should probably be called TQM.
13. Consider installing some formal procedures, and records, at least as far as control charts are concerned. Most customers will require some kind of record keeping and some kind of written procedures. Just remember, again, that too many formal procedures and records could

constitute a TQM rather than an SPC system (which, of course, can be very good).

14. Right after making the first improvement, start using supportive management activities, rather than autocratic ones (these are a "must" if SPC is to succeed). Start urging lower level managers, and finally all workers, to do the same. Begin to foster an atmosphere of trust, respect, and good feeling among all. Don't be fooled into thinking that this is already being done. Some of it may be, but probably not all (in fact, almost certainly not all).

HISTORY

Before the Industrial Revolution, quality was taken care of by the people who made the product. They built the entire product themselves, and therefore took pride in the fact that it was a quality product. Then came the Industrial Revolution. The entire product was no longer produced by one person. Instead, each person now did only a small portion, because it was much more efficient (saved money). The individual worker, then, was no longer responsible for the quality of the product. Therefore, a separate function was created, called quality control, to deal with this problem.

The first reaction to the quality problem was to impose a 100% inspection (every finished product would be thoroughly examined). This did not solve the problem, however. Not only was the cost of 100% inspection often prohibitive, it didn't seem to eliminate defective products from getting past the inspectors and thus to the customers (it especially did not eliminate the "mind numbing" problem caused by the worker doing the same small repetitive actions over and over and over).

Then, in the early 1920's, W. A. Shewhart of Bell Laboratories invented statistical quality control. It was actually a statistical process control system (controlling the process instead of the product) and it included the concept of letting the producers of the products (the workers) build in and measure their own quality. It also included control charts and statistical methods, which use the means of small samples (instead of 100% inspection) to measure and predict, rather than the actual measurements themselves. In this way, the resulting distribution is normal (when charted, they form a normal curve — see Chapter 3), which it has to be in order for the control charts to work. The reason for this is the mathematical relationship between the standard deviations (of the entire distribution and the sample distribution), called the "central limit theorem."

$$S_X = \sigma / \sqrt{n}$$

where

S_X = the standard deviation of the sample means

σ = the standard deviation of the individual values (also called the standard deviation of the universe or distribution from which the sample was taken)

n = the sample size.

The experience of quality practitioners over the intervening 70 years has shown conclusively the validity of Shewhart's theories. In fact, it is now acknowledged that a sampling procedure is vastly superior to 100% inspection in most cases (fewer errors are released to the customer than by a 100% inspection). Of course, some 100% inspections will always be necessary, especially of small amounts of very high-cost items.

Managers, however, quickly changed this to let a special function — the quality control department — use these statistical concepts, and to keep the workers concentrating on "things and costs" (productivity). Although foremen and others (especially the operators) were told they had responsibilities for quality, the realities were usually vastly different. For instance, the predicted amount of product was expected (by leaders) to be shipped, whether or not they were "quality" products, that is, whether or not they conformed to the specs. Quite naturally, this soon led to an almost total indifference to quality. Quality was, for the most part, given only lip service. SPC is attempting to change this.

It was during World War II that the viability of these concepts became apparent. The government, for the most part, forced the manufacturers to use statistical controls to ensure quality (Dr. W. Edwards Deming, a long time proponent of statistical process control, was instrumental in this effort). Although some of these SPC principles were adopted by American business at the end of the war, much of it was not. This was when Dr. Deming and Dr. Joseph M. Juran (and others) introduced Japan to SPC (Japan even has a national quality award called the "Deming" award, and Deming is fondly referred to as "Papa San Deming"). It was the Japanese who successfully implemented these procedures and proved their worth. They even invented some of their own, such as the Taguchi Design of Experiments and the Ishikawa Cause and Effect Diagram.

It was also about this time (the 1950's and 1960's) that several new motivational theories were introduced that had a profound effect on the emerging SPC system. One of SPC's concepts is that people work together in harmonious ways to accomplish quality (this is even more a TQM concept than an SPC one). And one of the most important SPC (and TQM) procedures used to ensure this is through the use of teams, called "team approach problem solving." It was the motivational theories of the 1950's and 1960's that seemed to show that this was possible — that quality and productivity could actually be increased together, and that people can be happy in this endeavor. No one now questions the truth and viability of these theories. (See Doty, 1996, Chapter 1.)

PROBLEM DEFINITION

The definition of a problem can be critical to its efficient solution (this is the essential first step of the so-called "scientific process"). The way we define our subject is crucial to the way we think about it which, in turn, is fundamental to how we apply it. This need for clear and understandable definition can be illustrated by the diagram (see Figure 1.1) of the "traditional" versus the SPC (Statistical Process Control) definition of "good" quality.

The past (traditional) definition of "good" quality has been "conformance to specifications." This occurs anywhere between the upper and lower specification limits (between the USL and the LSL). The newer SPC (Taguchi) definition is "as close to the target value as possible" (as close to the center of the specifications as possible). According to Genichi Taguchi, there is a "loss to society" that increases exponentially the further the characteristic is from the central, or target, value, even if still within the specification limits (due to many factors, not the least of which is excessive wear on mating parts).

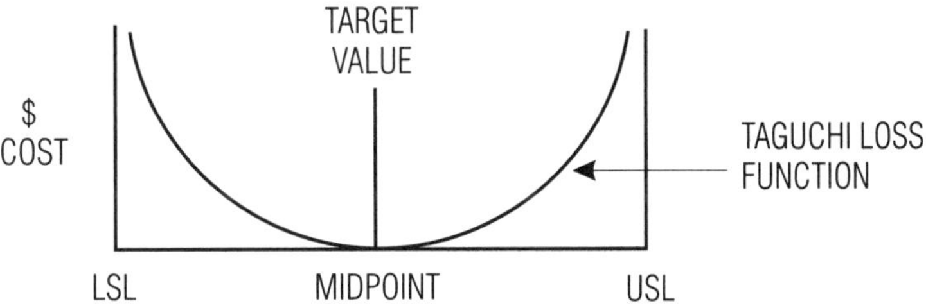

Figure 1.1. Comparison of traditional and SPC definitions of "good" quality.

Workers who are taught the "traditional" definition will think that products produced within the limits will be "good quality" even if very close to the limit. They will not realize that they may be actually producing fairly poor quality because their definition is flawed. The fact that the Japanese, who do work to the SPC definition (they get "as close to the center as possible"), forged ahead so dramatically on quality is a clear indication of the viability of the SPC, or Taguchi, approach.

QUALITY DEFINITIONS

Unfortunately, quality means different things to different people and, often, different things to the same people at different times and under different circumstances. Therefore, quality is often difficult, even at best, to precisely define. In general, a product is considered to be a quality product when it most effectively discharges the requirements of its function; when it meets its objectives with the least expenditure of time, effort, and money; and when it does what the customer wants it to do with no perceived problems. Defining and measuring these requirements, however, can be difficult and frustrating.

Quality, in the manufacturing setting at least, is the ability of the product and/or process to meet the various standards (the engineering specifications). The setting of the standards is the duty of Design Engineering. Measuring, comparing, and analyzing the quality characteristic, and its process, should be the duty of Production, with assistance (especially in the use of statistics) from Quality Control and/or Statistical Process Control. It is the duty, then, of production personnel to properly manufacture the product to the standards set by design and, when informed by quality analysis (their own or SPC's), apply corrective action to quality deviations. Quality Control, in an SPC setting, assists and trains the production personnel, does sophisticated analyses for production and for management, and performs periodic audits on every aspect of the quality program. Inspectors usually report to production, but they can be part of quality control.

Quality also includes the little things that add to comfort (such as ease of operation, ease of maintenance, etc.). Some of these things are: trouble/diagnostic lights, interlocks to prevent inadvertent activation or inactivation (such as "can't start the engine until the gear is in park, or the brake is on"), computer discs in permanent jackets for safety, etc. Quality includes the identification, and implementation, of these things even when not specifically perceived by the customer (if not done, someone else soon will and take your customers away!).

Quality is also the confidence the customer has in the company. It is everyone caring about what they do, and what they, and especially the company, have to offer the customer. It is such things as: caring that the customer gets the finest product possible, returning phone calls quickly, processing paperwork accurately, keeping a clean workplace, dealing with clients cheerfully, etc. There are many others, but these are presented to emphasize the kind of attitude needed — a quality attitude. This quality attitude is probably more TQM than SPC. Nevertheless, it is the kind of attitude that SPC practitioners must cultivate. In TQM, this kind of attitude is usually quite formal and obvious; everyone is made aware of it, and assisted to have it and increase it. In SPC, however, this kind of attitude tends to be somewhat informal, with little or no formal systems or people assigned to it. Employees will tend to not use this attitude, however, or their innate ingenuity and knowledge, if they are not reasonably free (or at least perceive themselves to be), if they are not shown a reasonable amount of respect and courtesy, and if they do not perceive their efforts as being appreciated.

In SPC, statistics are used to identify special (assignable) causes of variation in a process. Once the variations are identified by SPC, it is up to the various people involved to use their creativity and ingenuity to correct these variations. This is SPC's way of controlling the products. If the processes are in control, it is assumed that the products produced from these processes will also be in control (this does *not* assume that the products will meet the specifications — see Chapter 6). Thus, instead of controlling the products with mostly 100% inspections, the processes are controlled with sampling procedures (a much cheaper, and potentially surer and longer lasting, control system).

The main goal of SPC is customer satisfaction. The focus is to increase this satisfaction with a disciplined approach to continuous improvement involving any and all functions of the firm and any and all available tools.

RESPONSIBILITY FOR QUALITY

Although quality is the responsibility of everyone, it is not enough just to say so. Quality responsibilities must be carefully defined and then clearly assigned so that everyone is thoroughly aware of his or her specific duties as regards quality. Otherwise the responsibility for quality tends to become diffused and everyone tends to expect everyone else to control the quality. In this way, a policy of "everyone responsible for quality" tends to become, informally, "everyone else but me is responsible for quality," and then "no one but Quality Control is responsible for quality." It is this deterioration of quality responsibilities, in the past, that the new SPC philosophy is designed to eliminate (one of the things, at least).

In general, the SPC system expects the operator, the person actually making the product, to assume more of the quality decision making. With SPC, this is somewhat understood by all, and informally practiced by all (with TQM, however, this type of authority structure is organized, with formal rules and practices). Thus the operator assumes a level of responsibility, control, and authority seldom, if ever, known in the old quality philosophy. Production supervisors, instead of being "arbiters" of quality, now become just another resource for the operator to use in order to improve quality.

With more decision making power comes more control which, in the opinion of most behavioral experts, leads to increased worker satisfaction and decreased job stress. Workers who are more satisfied with their jobs, and who are happier and calmer (less stressed), SPC contends, will almost always produce increased product quality, increased output, and decreased costs.

HOW MUCH QUALITY?

The ultimate quality goal is zero errors. In the world in which we live this is really not possible — errors will occur sooner or later. However, we can try. That is what SPC is about. Because of this attitude (that errors will eventually occur), many quality systems in the past have assumed 99% quality as a goal (a 99% error-free environment). If we were to define "good quality" as a 99.9% error-free environment (even better than past assumptions), this would seem almost perfect and certainly would appear to be sufficient. But this means, in certain key areas:

- 20,000 wrong drug prescriptions each year
- 4 wrong numbers on each page of the telephone book
- 730 short or long landings per year at each major airport in the country
- 140,000,000 lost pieces of mail per year
- 26,000 wrong surgical operations per year
- 19,000 babies dropped at birth each year
- 193,000,000 checks deducted from wrong accounts per year
- heart fails to beat 32,000 times per year (it only takes one failure to kill, although the heart can usually be restarted each time if a physician happens to be at hand with the proper equipment).

Obviously even 99.9% quality is not acceptable in many cases. Unfortunately, modern complex high technology demands this kind of quality even in many (or most?) manufacturing systems.

To illustrate the problem further, suppose that control chart limits were to be set at the specification limits. Control charts assume a 3 sigma (3σ), or 99.73% good quality (see Chapter 3). For a product with 1,000 parts, each controlled to this level of quality, there will only be one good unit for every 15 produced ($1/0.9973^{1000} = 14.9$). This kind of problem can be solved using capability (C_p) ratios (see Chapter 6).

Phil Crosby, one of the three "gurus" of modern Quality Control in the United States (the other two are W. Edwards Deming and Joseph M. Juran), has suggested that we act as if only 100% quality is acceptable (he calls this Zero Defects). Most quality professionals tend to reject this idea because the facts of existence mandate that errors will certainly occur eventually. Over time, it is obviously impossible to live an error-free life and to produce totally error-free products.

Yet perhaps Crosby's theory can have some merit if applied as an attitude rather than as a demand on nature. His philosophy seems to imply that this attitude (always striving and hoping for zero defects) will tend to keep mistakes to a minimum. Certainly, the past idea, that mistakes must occur and we must design for them in our systems, has not worked. Without a zero defects type attitude, errors tend to become institutionalized and to gradually increase over time. This institutionalization of errors appears to be exactly what has happened in the United States over the past 80 years, and what has contributed to the decline in quality in U.S. products in that time. What is more, the Japanese, in their insistence on higher and higher quality, appear to have substantiated Crosby's theory. This, and other sources of SPC activity, have pretty well confirmed that a "defect-free" attitude can lead to long-term increases in both quality and productivity.

SPC AND VARIATION

The purpose of SPC is to assist in the production of quality products and services. Bad products and services are caused by variation, and variation is produced by the process that made the product or service. Therefore, SPC concentrates on the process, and assists in reducing process variation (it is assumed that if the process is perfected, so will the products produced on it). When this is done, the distance between control limits will get smaller and smaller, the control limits will get closer and closer to the central value, and the standard deviation of the process is reduced. This does *not* mean that the engineering specification limits will be reduced. Control chart limits have nothing to do with specification limits, or vice versa. However, they can, and should, be compared (how and why this is done is discussed in Chapter 6).

For quality control purposes, the causes of variation are almost always classified as assignable (special) causes or chance causes. Chance causes are those that are small in magnitude and present a stable picture of variation where no long-term patterns are discernible. Assignable causes, on the other hand, are more readily recognized through one or more of a group of different types of long-term trends and patterns (see Chapter 6). They are assumed to be correctable, and their identification and correction is one of the most important objectives of SPC and Quality Control.

When variation causes are identified, it is up to operators, engineering, foremen, management, etc., to reduce them. A knowledge of the process would seem critical in reducing any errors caused by the process. All approaches to reducing variation will cause an improvement in the process. This is one of the most important aspects of SPC — the constant reduction of variation and the constant improvement of processes. Chapter 6 gives a list of variation causes.

THE COST OF QUALITY

Much of this section has been derived from Crosby, 1979; Juran and Gryna, 1980; and Doty, 1996. There are two ways to look at costs. One is to examine how they impact on production, that is, on the cost of producing a product. The other is to analyze costs from the standpoint of how they affect quality. This second way is called "Quality Costs," and is the subject of this section.

Traditionally, quality costs have been looked upon as a necessary evil — a necessary cost of doing business. Because of this, management has viewed the costs of quality as necessary overhead that must be reduced. However, this is a big mistake. It may be necessary, for instance, to actually increase some costs in order to decrease others more (for instance, costs associated with reducing scrap should be increased until it exactly offsets the cost of scrap). Also, it could be, at times, that an increase in the costs to one department will lead to a greater decrease in total costs to the firm (for instance, an increase in purchasing costs that leads to an even greater decrease in production costs). If department managers are only held responsible for their own costs, and not for the firm's total costs, they will tend to optimize their own costs at the expense of total cost (this is known as suboptimizing; some call it lazy management). The best way out of this dilemma is to analyze costs in relation to their impact on quality, and for everybody to work together to minimize total costs to the firm.

For best analysis, quality costs must be divided into their various categories so that the factors that affect these costs can be more properly examined. These categories are: prevention, appraisal, and failure costs. Failure costs are further subdivided into internal failures and external failures (external failures take place in the field after the customer uses the product). Failure costs are the most undesirable of all, especially external failure costs because of their direct effect on customer satisfaction. In general, prevention and appraisal costs have a direct, and opposite, effect on failure costs. As prevention and appraisal costs increase, failure costs tend to decrease, and vice versa. The goal should be to increase prevention and appraisal costs until they exactly offset the failure costs.

Managers can control prevention and appraisal costs, but failure costs are directly related to the quality of the product. Prevention and appraisal costs are considered to be controllable (direct control, that is) but failure costs are not (they are determined, to a great extent, by the amount of prevention and appraisal costs expended). Prevention and appraisal costs must be controlled in such a way that their increase results in a maximum reduction of failure costs. It would be ideal, of course, if reductions in failure costs more than offset increases in prevention and appraisal costs. Since this kind of maximum effect seldom occurs, there is almost always room for improvement in all cost categories.

One of the problems with controlling quality costs is the difficulty in identifying and quantifying them in most firms. Costs must be measured in order to be properly managed. If you can't measure it, you don't really know how much it is, and you most certainly won't be able to effectively control it. In the past, most charts of accounts (Accounting's way of summarizing and controlling costs) did not separate costs according to their impact on quality. Instead, they were added in with other cost categories. Thus the separation and identification of these costs become a major problem to the quality analyst. Of course, if Accounting can be prevailed upon to separate these costs in the chart of accounts (change the chart of accounts), this problem would disappear. But this, then, would present Accounting with a major difficulty, as it will usually require extensive changes in their cost collecting procedures (also, many quality costs are quite difficult to measure). The solution to this problem is seldom easy.

Prevention Costs

These are the costs of designing, implementing, and maintaining a quality system, and the costs of all activities associated with creating the error prevention activities that are applied during the business cycle. It is important to clearly distinguish between prevention and appraisal costs. Prevention costs are associated with the *creation* and *design* of cost control systems, while appraisal costs are the costs of *using* those systems to detect errors. Some of the more important prevention cost categories involved are as follows:

1. The development of the quality, inspection, and reliability plans, and the data gathering and analysis system associated with these plans. Only the development of, and any subsequent refinements or alterations to, the system are prevention costs. The costs of running the system are appraisal costs.
2. Design and development of quality control equipment (including any subsequent upgrading, redesigning, and/or improvement). The costs of maintaining and using the equipment are appraisal costs.
3. SPC and other Quality Control training. The costs of ongoing quality activities are appraisal and/or failure costs.
4. Zero defects and other error prevention programs.
5. Design review.
6. Product qualification.
7. Quality orientation for new employees.
8. Supplier evaluations — initial qualification appraisal.
9. Process capability studies (see Chapter 6).

10. Quality system audits.
11. Preventive maintenance.
12. Acceptance planning.
13. Specification and drawing reviews.

Appraisal Costs

These include all costs resulting from assessing and analyzing the condition of the product and measuring and evaluating its conformance to standards. Appraisal cost categories include the following:

1. Inspecting and testing incoming material and periodically auditing the supplier's quality control system.
2. Inspection and testing of the product during production.
3. Product quality audits.
4. Equipment calibration and maintenance.
5. Product acceptance.
6. Status measuring, analysis, and reporting.

Internal Failure Costs

These costs occur when product defects are identified prior to transfer of ownership (prior to the customer receiving the product). Internal failure costs include the following:

1. Scrap.
2. Rework.
3. Determining the nature and cause of the defect (failure analysis).
4. Reinspection.
5. Analyses of supplier problems, and supplier material faults and/or failures.
6. Downgrading of the product if it is sold at a discount due to defects or failure.
7. Redesigning the product due to internal failures (usually measured by engineering change orders, purchasing change orders, and/or corrective action costs).

External Failure Costs

These are the costs that occur after the customer receives the product. External failures have a direct effect on customer satisfaction, and therefore on sales. Therefore, any failure or defect reduction system must first concentrate on the reduction, and control, of these most critical defect types before extending the control to other areas. External defects include the following:

1. Adjustment for complaints.
2. Handling, repairs, and replacement of returned products.
3. Warranty expenses.
4. Liability and litigation expense.
5. Consumer relations.
6. Redesigning the product due to external failures (usually measured by engineering change orders, purchasing change orders, and/or corrective action costs).

CONTROLLING QUALITY COSTS

For the most part, quality costs are difficult to relate directly to profits. Just how a particular quality cost affects the profit picture is usually difficult to determine. Several techniques have evolved that attempt to solve this problem, but none of them alone is completely effective. However, if they are all used carefully, along with judicious management judgment, quality costs can be reasonably controlled while, at the same time, keeping profits effectively maximized.

1. Comparative analysis with other companies. In this kind of analysis, individual comparisons must be made as well as total costs. Unfortunately, a total breakdown of costs from another company must be available in order for proper comparisons to be made, and this type of breakdown is difficult to obtain. This concept has been expanded into a system of total comparison now widely known as "benchmarking," which is one of the judging standards of the annual Malcolm Baldridge quality award.
2. Analyze the interrelationships among cost categories. The ideal is to have the total of the prevention and appraisal costs exactly equal the failure costs. If the sum of the prevention and appraisal costs is less than the failure costs, quality improvement activities are insufficient and should be increased. Of course, the sum of prevention and appraisal costs must never be greater than the failure costs.
3. Optimize individual costs. In general, this can be done when no profitable projects for reducing these costs (and maintaining long-range profits at the same time) can be readily identified, and when quality costs are controlled by sound budgeting. Remember that optimization can mean either minimizing or maximizing, and that some quality costs must be kept rather high in order to keep failures at a minimum.
4. Compare to prior history. If quality costs steadily decline from cost period to cost period (while sales and profits are increasing and customer complaints are decreasing), it can probably be assumed that quality costs are being properly minimized.

— Chapter 2 —

CONTROL CHART THEORY

A control chart is a graphical display of a measure of a quality characteristic (such as weight, length, temperature, waiting time, typing errors, etc.) over time. The measurement of the characteristic is plotted on the vertical axis, with the sample number (also called subgroup or subsample) on the horizontal axis. Samples should be recorded (plotted) as they are taken so that the plot shows progression, patterns, etc., over time. In this way, the operator, and any others that are involved, receive information about problems as they occur.

All control charts have a midpoint (or centerline) which corresponds to the process average (the mean of the normal distribution — the μ of Chapter 3), and an upper and lower limit which correspond to ± three standard deviations ($\pm 3\sigma$) from this midpoint. How these chart values are determined will be explained later in Chapters 4 and 5. The central value is usually plotted as a horizontal solid line, and upper and lower control limits as horizontal dotted lines. However, some analysts like to reverse this procedure and plot the limit lines as solid with the central line dotted. Patterns in the chart's plotted values are used to evaluate the process (see Chapter 6).

CONTROL CHART CONCEPTS

1. SYMBOLS. Symbols are used in the charts as a shorthand means of conveying information. A bar above a symbol, such as $\overline{X}$ (pronounced X-bar) means "the average of" (X-bar, then, means the average of the X's). Two bars above a symbol, such as $\overline{\overline{X}}$ (pronounced X-double-bar)

means the average of the averages (*X*-double-bar, then, means "the average of the *X*-bars"). The lower case *p*, in the *p* charts, means percent defective (this is actually a probability value, that is, the probability that any one unit in the sample is defective, but it is better to think of it as percent defective). The *c*, in the *u* and *c* charts, means number of defects, and the *u* means average number of defects; n = the subgroup size; Σn = the total beginning sample size; and m = the number of subgroups (therefore, $mn = \Sigma n$ when n is constant — when n is the same for all subgroups). Other symbols are mostly mathematical and have the usual mathematical values.

2. VARIABLES VERSUS ATTRIBUTES. A variable refers to a continuous characteristic (length, width, temperature, hardness, errors per page, etc.), while an attribute is a discrete characteristic (number of items not in conformance to specifications). In quality control, variables are measured and attributes are counted. A continuous characteristic can, theoretically, take on any value (there can be, theoretically, an infinite number of possible measurements between 1 and 2, 2 and 3, etc.), while a discrete characteristic, as far as quality control is concerned, is a counting number only (1, 2, 3, etc.). It is the actual measurements (actually, averages of subgroups of these measurements), or some coded variation of them that are plotted on the variables charts. In attributes charts, it is the average number of nonconformances, or nonconforming items, that are charted (in manufacturing, a nonconformance is called a defect while a nonconforming item is called a defective).
3. TYPES OF CONTROL CHARTS. There are at least 27 different types of control charts. They are divided into control charts for variables and control charts for attributes. Attributes control charts are further divided into attributes control charts for defective units (*p* charts), and attributes control charts for defects (*u* and *c* charts). Variables control charts control on actual measurements (actually, the means of small sample sizes), while attributes control charts control on counts (the number of defective units for *p* charts and the number of defects for *u* and *c* charts).
4. PLOTTING. All variables charts, except for zero-base coding charts, are used for plotting only one quality characteristic of one product on the same chart (even with zero-base coding charts, the same characteristic must be used for the different products charted). Any of the attributes charts (*p*, *u*, *c*, or any variation of these three) can be used for plotting a single characteristic, many characteristics, a single characteristic of many products, many characteristics of many products, an entire plant, or labor or administration performance.

5. PATTERNS. This is how control charts work; patterns in the chart's plotted points are examined for information and clues leading to problems, causes, and possible solutions. Attribute patterns can only provide nonconformance information since they only record information outside the specification limits. If these attributes charts also have a place for recording causes (or types of defectives), then they can also provide an almost automatic Pareto analysis (see Chapter 7) about causes of nonconformances. Variables charts, on the other hand, can show patterns within the specification limits so that possible problems can be highlighted, and hopefully prevented, before they become nonconformances (attributes charts cannot do this). See Chapter 6 for a discussion on pattern analysis.
6. DEFECTIVES AND DEFECTS. In quality control, a quality characteristic that measures outside the specification limits is called a "defect," or nonconformance. A unit which has at least one of these quality characteristics (at least one defect) is called a "defective" (examples of quality characteristics are: length, weight, color, hardness, errors per line, etc.). Therefore, a defective (a nonconforming unit) can have many defects. (The terms nonconformance and nonconforming unit are much more meaningful when quality is applied to nonmanufacturing.)
7. DATA CONVERSION. Variables data (measurements) can easily be converted into attributes data (counts) just by comparing them to the specification limits (any measurement outside the tolerance spread, or specification limits, is defective or nonconforming). It is also possible to convert attributes into variables data (by judging on a scale of 1 to 5, 1 to 10, etc.), but this is much more difficult — so difficult, in fact, that it is almost never done (although some nonmanufacturing data are handled this way).
8. PRODUCT VERSUS PROCESS. A fundamental principle of SPC is that emphasis is on controlling the process, not the product (that is the reason for the word "process" in the title rather than "quality"). If the process is in control, it is much more probable that products produced from that process will also be in control. Thus, application of control charts, as well as all other principles of SPC, requires a thorough knowledge and understanding of the processes involved in producing the product. The relationship between product and process, and the way this is used to control product quality, is further explained in Chapter 6.
9. VARIATION. The basic purpose of all quality control charts is to reduce variation (reduce the standard deviation so that the limits get closer to the chart centerline). The way they do this is to provide

information on the types and causes of variation so that these causes can be eliminated (or, at least, their effects can be substantially reduced). The first way that variation is reduced is to correct quality problems — to eliminate causes that keep the process from being in control. The second way that variation is reduced is to change the process so that it produces a better product faster (although a changed process does not have to reduce the variation, it usually does). Both of these activities (correction and change) improve the process, which then tends to improve the products of that process. The relation between control charts and these two variation reduction activities (corrective actions and process changes) is thoroughly examined in Chapter 6, which also has a listing of variation causes.

10. MANAGEMENT CONTROL. In addition to reducing variation, attributes charts can also be used to supply control information to management (percent defectives per process, per product, per plant, etc.). Attributes control charts, then, have two broad purposes: to provide overall quality information to management (percent defectives for a particular process, for an entire product line, for an entire plant, etc.) and to provide information for the correction of problems and the improvement of quality (nonconformances and automatic Pareto information). Attributes charts should contain an organized type of information, an almost automatic Pareto analysis section (see the charts in Chapter 5), that helps to provide this information.
11. LONG PROCESS TIMES. Long process times present an especially difficult problem for attributes charts. When process times are long, it takes too long for an attributes chart to signal a possible out-of-control situation. Also, when process times are very long, each subgroup may take more than one day to complete. One way out of this problem is to use one day's production as the subgroup size (people usually have a difficult time remembering what happened more than one day at a time, anyway). The subgroup size, then, would almost never be constant, and a variable or an average p chart must be used. Also, 100% inspection would almost always be necessary (especially when the number of defectives becomes quite low) even though the day's production would be treated as a sample on the charts (this makes no difference as far as chart analysis is concerned). Chart patterns can still be used to analyze for problems, causes, and solutions. This is also explained in Chapter 5 in conjunction with the average p chart.

CONTROL CHART CONSTRUCTION

There are ten steps in constructing, and using, control charts.

1. Select the quality characteristic.
2. Develop the quality plan.
3. Choose the type of chart (variables or attributes).
4. Choose the control chart.
5. Determine the frequency.
6. Determine the sample size.
7. Collect the data.
8. Determine the chart midpoint and control limits.
9. Construct the chart.
10. Continue to use the chart.

In actuality, and to conform most closely to statistical rationale, a trial control chart should be calculated first, the outside values omitted (if they are found to relate to nonconformances), and a revised chart then constructed. However, this book will not do this. Only the trial chart will be used and no revised chart will be calculated, since the trial chart is perfectly adequate for controlling the process anyway. In actual practice, the chart is revised monthly anyway. Also, many computer programs do not recognize revised charts.

Select the Quality Characteristic

Quality characteristics are chosen for control chart analysis because they are important ones that can affect the performance of the product (critical or major characteristics); or because they are causing, or are central to, a manufacturing or quality problem; or because of contract requirements.

It is best, when starting out, to choose a product and a product characteristic that will be easy to correct and/or improve, and where costs can easily be reduced. In this way, the workers can see an immediate return for their efforts, and be more disposed to continue the program.

Although control charts can be placed anywhere they are needed, the best place, and the first that should be considered, is at any point where inspections are being performed. These points should be precisely located on manufacturing flow charts (see Chapter 7) and the production work order. (Normally, the production work order contains all the details of the production plan and the quality plan. However, each of these plans can be separate documents.) The general rule should be to inspect as little as possible while still ensuring product quality. Although it is fairly easy to determine where to place a manufacturing control chart (mostly because of inspection points), this is not the case with nonmanufacturing.

Some of the more important considerations for selecting an inspection point, and therefore a place to put a control chart, are as follows.

1. Inspect after operations that are likely to produce defective items to ensure that no more work will be performed on faulty items.
2. Inspect before costly operations so that the costly work will not be performed on defective parts.
3. Inspect prior to those operations where faulty items are likely to cause production problems (such as breaking or jamming the machine).
4. Inspect before operations that might cover up a defect or cannot be undone (such as painting, assembly, welding, etc.).
5. Inspect first and last pieces on automatic and semiautomatic machines, but rarely in between.
6. Inspect finished products. Remember that the customer is the next inspector and that a satisfied customer is the best job insurance.
7. Inspect before storage.
8. Use control charts at the beginning of a new program, process, or product for all important operations and/or product characteristics and then remove them as they are found to be unnecessary (although it may be useful to leave them so that the personnel involved can see the results of their efforts, and so that the operator is more motivated to continue quality improvements).
9. Use a team of engineers and/or operators to determine when, where, and how to use the charts.

Develop the Quality Plan

The purpose of quality planning should be to establish an economic balance between the cost of measurement and the value of the measurement (as defined, usually, by product acceptance and customer satisfaction). In general, quality plans define the inspection/testing points and methods, the type of measurement, the sample size, time and place of each inspection, and who will do the inspection and sampling. They also reference specific inspection instructions and acceptance criteria.

Quality plans, along with production plans, are primarily documented on the work order (although they can be separate documents). The work order lists all production steps and inspection points; references the drawings, specifications, procedures, instructions, and standards that contain information required for production and inspection; and gives a step-by-step procedure for production of the product.

Choose the Type of Chart (Variables or Attributes)

This choice will depend on the nature of the measurement and the cost involved. Although variables charts are preferred (they provide more information), they are expensive. However, attributes charts have several disadvantages not shared by variables charts. First, though they can provide hints and even fairly strong evidence of possible causes of nonconformance, they seldom provide the detailed information often needed for a complete solution. They can never, for instance, provide information on the process patterns that occur between the specification limits; it takes a variables chart to do this. Second, they do not react to process changes until after the changes occur and the process is out of control. Variables charts, on the other hand, can indicate shifts and potential problems before defects are actually produced, before the process deteriorates to an out-of-control status. Finally, attributes charts seldom provide the definitive information needed for good process improvement programs. Mostly this is because of the lack of in-control patterns from measurements that fall between the specification limits (which are, of course, provided by variables charts only).

In general, variables data can easily be converted into attributes data (any item that measures outside the specifications is defective), but it is much more difficult to convert attributes data into variables data. Attributes can be converted into variables by use of an interval scale (judge the effectiveness or "degree" of quality on a scale of 1 to 10, for instance), but this practice is seldom necessary or useful (except occasionally in the use of SPC for nonmanufacturing or service processes). Even when used, its effectiveness is suspect because of the subjective "judgment" that must be employed. Interval scale "judgments" require a great deal of training so that all inspectors involved will be judging from the same base, that is, the same perspectives and understandings. Definitions of each scale interval (for instance, what constitutes a "1," a "2," a "3," etc.) must be understood the same way by all (see Chapter 5 for an example of a variables chart using attributes data).

Variables Chart

A variables chart should be considered in the following instances.

- The process is obviously in trouble; it cannot produce to the tolerances on a consistent basis.
- Destructive or expensive testing is being used.
- Sampling further along in the manufacturing process can be reduced by a more positive control at an earlier stage.
- Attributes control charts have shown a problem to exist but the solution is difficult or unknown.
- There are difficult problem processes with tight specifications, overlapping assembly tolerances, expensive materials, etc.

- The critical characteristic is measurable.
- The customer and/or contract requires it.

Attributes Chart

An attributes chart should be considered in the following instances.

- Operators have a high degree of control over assignable causes.
- Assembly operations are complex.
- Quality can only be measured in terms of good or bad, or measurement data are otherwise unobtainable.
- Historical information is needed for management review (an overall management control device).
- Many characteristics must be measured at one time.
- Cost of measurement is high.
- Production runs are large.

Choose the Control Chart

This requires a knowledge and understanding of what each chart is, what it can do, and where it can be used. Frequently more than one chart can be effectively used in any one situation, and the one finally used is often due as much to individual taste as to any theoretical consideration. The conditions under which each chart can be used, and a description of how and when they should be used, is given for each chart shown in Chapters 4 and 5.

Determine the Frequency

A good rule of thumb to use for determining the variables sampling frequency is adapted from MIL-STD-414. In general, the number to be inspected per lot is as follows.

Lot Size	Percentage
1. 60 to 300	10%
2. 301 to 1,000	5%
3. 1,001 to 5,000	2%
4. Over 5,000	1%

Although a lot is normally considered to be one day's production, it can be expanded to as much as one week under special circumstances. The main reason for limiting the lot size to one day's production is to facilitate process analysis and assignable cause identification. People tend to forget the details of what happened after more than one day has elapsed.

For a daily production of 200 (using the above rule of thumb), 20 units should be inspected each day. If the subgroup size is to be 4 (always use a subgroup size of 4, if possible), there should then be a minimum of 5 samples of 4 measured and recorded per day. The 5 subgroups, of course, must be taken at random, or as randomly as possible (although they must be plotted in the order of measurement to preserve the time frame). The reason for this is that the sampling time is often critical to correction and/or improvement procedures. The conclusions reached via this logic can, and often should, be adjusted by management to satisfy other considerations (inspection and product cost, product worth, product and characteristic importance, production schedules, degree of production disruption caused by the measurement process, etc.).

Attributes can be counted once each day, or in relation to each work order, but the actual frequency will depend on the lots, the production plans, and any other consideration that affects the counting procedure.

Determine the Sample Size

There are two different sample sizes — the start-up size and the subgroup size. The start-up sample size should always be 25 subgroups, if possible. The subgroup size is the amount measured at one time. For variables charts, the units should be measured consecutively as produced, if possible (if this is not possible, the period-of-time method can be used, where a subgroup is chosen from all the product produced during a preset period of time). Since attributes charts only record the number of nonconformances, they can be counted at any time.

Both subgroups and start-up samples are statistical samples (subgroups are also called subsamples). However, it is best to think of the plotted amount as a subgroup and the start-up amount as a sample, so as not to confuse them with each other (although in actual practice a subgroup is called a sample after the initial start-up phase is completed). The recommended subgroup size will be given in Chapters 4 and 5 for each chart presented.

Collect the Data

Any sample, in order to properly represent the population characteristics, must be unbiased, that is, random. In meeting this criterion, subgroups can be selected from product produced at one time (instant time) or over a period of time. The instant-time method is preferred because it provides a time reference for pinpointing assignable causes and because it is more sensitive to process changes. However, some products and/or characteristics, by their nature, may demand the period-of-time method. The rule here is to use the instant-time method unless circumstances make this impossible.

If the instant-time method is used, the inspector measures several subgroups of parts at random times during the day (that is, each subgroup is randomly chosen, but the subgroup itself consists of consecutive units produced at the random time chosen). If the period-of-time method is used, each subgroup unit is chosen randomly from all the parts produced during that period of time. After the measurements (called observations) are made, the mean of the subgroup is calculated and graphed. Because of the Central Limit Theorem, only the averages are graphed, never the individual values (except for some specialized charts).

If the purpose is to gather enough data for construction of the control chart, the measurements are recorded until enough observations are made, after which the chart is made and then the subgroup averages recorded. Data are usually gathered by the inspection function as a normal part of their regular duties, or by the operators themselves if a complete SPC program is in effect.

The data can be collected and tabled, either vertically or horizontally. In actual practice, the data are usually entered directly onto the chart in a space provided.

Determine the Chart Midpoint and Control Limits

In order to more perfectly conform to statistical procedure, a trial chart should first be determined, all outside values discarded (if they prove to be caused by a process problem), and a revised chart constructed. The revised chart, then, would be the one used. However, many programs do not recognize revised charts (they just use the trial charts), and trial charts are completely adequate for controlling the process anyway. Also, charts are revised on a monthly basis anyway. Therefore, only trial charts will be used here.

If the midpoint and limits have been properly determined and the process is properly operating, 99.73% of all subgroup averages will fall between the chart control limits (not specification limits). Any one average, in other words, has only a 0.27% chance (100 - 99.73%) of being outside of these limits (actually, the chance is one-half of 0.27, or 0.135% that the measurement will be above the upper limit and 0.135% that it will be below the lower). Because of this small chance, any values above the upper limit or below the lower limit are assumed to have assignable (special) causes (the process is assumed to be out of control), and a search instituted to find them. If no cause can be found, of course, the data point is assumed to be one with a very small chance (0.27%) to be outside the limit.

The method for determining these three values will be given for each chart presented (see Chapters 4 and 5).

Construct the Charts

All statistical quality control charts have a midpoint (centerline) which corresponds to the process average (the μ of Chapter 3) and an upper and lower limit which correspond to ± three standard deviations (the σ of Chapter 3) from this midpoint or centerline. These chart values are determined from special tables. The procedures for how this is accomplished will be shown with each control chart of Chapters 4 and 5.

Control charts are just graphs of the subgroup means (averages) with the central value shown as a solid line and each limit shown as a dotted line (a very few specialized charts chart the measured value only). Actually, control charts are just upended normal curves with the mean and 6 sigma limits extended ($+3\sigma$, or +3 standard deviations, above the mean for the upper control limit and -3σ below the mean for the lower control limit).

All quality control charts are constructed from the basic normal curve model (Gaussian). Control charts for variables (*X*-bar,*R*, *X*-bar,*s*, etc.) use the normal curve model direct while attributes charts use the normal curve approximation to the binomial (*p* charts) and the normal curve approximation to the Poisson (*u* and *c* charts). Special formulas and tables have been derived to simplify these calculations.

Continue to Use the Charts

Once the revised control chart is constructed, all subgroup means, even the out-of-control values, are entered (plotted) on the chart, and the chart is displayed conspicuously at the job site. Samples of the same size (the subgroup size) are measured periodically, and charting is continued. Thus the chart presents a continuous picture of the process quality and provides a foundation for quality and process improvement. The means of accomplishing this, called Process Analysis, will be explained in Chapter 6. It is best for the operator to measure, chart, and assist in the correction of problems.

— Chapter 3 —

THE NORMAL CURVE

Since the normal curve (also called the normal distribution or Guassian) forms the theoretical foundation for all control charts, this chapter will explain the most important aspects of the normal curve (at least those that affect quality and control charts).

THE UNIVERSE AND A SAMPLE

A universe (also called a population) is a collection of all possible values. The average weight of all United States citizens would be an example of a universe characteristic. A sample, on the other hand, is a group of these values. A group of United States citizens (say, 1000) chosen at random would be an example of a sample characteristic. If the sample is measured and used correctly, and if it is large enough, its average will almost always be close to the universe average.

The concept of randomness is important in this situation. Randomness means that all members of the universe have an equal chance of being chosen for the sample. Control charts use procedures that ensure this randomness. In statistical parlance, a random sample is said to be nonbiased, while a nonrandom sample is said to be biased. Biased samples cannot be effectively used in normal curve calculations.

Characteristics of the universe are called parameters while characteristics of samples are called statistics. All processes are universes, so process characteristics are parameters (that is why process characteristics are referred to as process parameters). Symbols are used to represent the more important characteristics. The universe mean is called μ (the lower case Greek letter mu) while the universe standard deviation is called σ (the lower case Greek letter sigma). A sample mean, on the other hand, is called $\overline{X}$ (or *X*-bar) and a sample standard deviation is called s. The number of all members of a universe or a sample is called n (just which one it refers to, sample or universe, must almost always have to be inferred from the problem, although it is almost always obvious). And the number of samples is called m. These values are characteristics of all groups (whether a universe or a sample) and are given special attention, as they are used repeatedly in all control charts.

CENTRAL TENDENCY AND DISPERSION

The central tendency refers to the tendency of all measurements of the same characteristic to be the same — to be close to the center. Sometimes this tendency is strong with the values close to the center, while at other times this tendency is weak with the values far from the center. The mean, or arithmetic average, is the most important central tendency for statistics (although there are others).

Dispersion refers to the tendency to be different. When this tendency is strong, the measurements are far from the center. When this tendency is weak, the measurements cluster about the central value. Obviously, these two measures (central tendency and dispersion) are opposite of each other. There are two main dispersion values — the range and the standard deviation. Another measure of the dispersion, the variance, is just the square of the standard deviation. It is used extensively in DOE, but not at all in control charts.

When the distributions are normal, strong central tendencies and weak dispersions are characterized by high, peaked curves (and called leptokurtic). Weak central tendencies and strong dispersions are characterized by low, flat curves (and called platykurtic). Kurtic is a measure of peakedness, and has some importance in some applications, although not in this text.

The Mean

The mean, or arithmetic average, is a central tendency. It is the average of all values, and is represented mathematically by the formula:

$$\overline{X} = \Sigma X/n$$

where $\overline{X}$ is the mean, Σ is the upper case Greek letter sigma and means "the sum of," X is a measurement, and n is the number of measurements.

There are other central tendency values, but the mean is almost universally used in this situation. The other central values are rarely used in control charts.

Suppose the following 4 measurements are made: 2.12, 2.23, 2.50, 2.35. The mean is:

$$\overline{X} = \Sigma X / n = (2.12 + 2.23 + 2.50 + 2.35) / 4 = 2.30.$$

The Range

The range is a dispersion measurement, and is defined as the distance from the smallest to the largest value. The formula is:

$$R = \mathrm{H} - \mathrm{L} = X_{\mathrm{H}} - X_{\mathrm{L}}$$

where R is the range, H is the high value, L is the low value, and X is a measurement. The range is important for determining cells and for constructing X-bar,R type control charts.

Suppose the following 4 measurements are made: 2.12, 2.23, 2.50, 2.35. The range is:

$$R = \mathrm{H} - \mathrm{L} = X_{\mathrm{H}} - X_{\mathrm{L}} = 2.50 - 2.12 = 0.38.$$

The Standard Deviation

The standard deviation is another important dispersion measure, and is defined as the average distance from the mean. The universe formula is:

$$\sigma = \sqrt{\Sigma(X - \mu)^2 / n}$$

where $\sqrt{\ }$ is the square root sign, Σ is the "sum of" sign, X is an individual measurement, μ is the mean, n is the number of measurements, and σ (the Greek letter sigma) is the universe standard deviation.

The sample formula (s) divides by n -1 because of the normal bias caused by small sample sizes. The formula is:

$$s = \sqrt{\Sigma(X - \overline{X})^2 / (n - 1)}.$$

In actuality, it is another formula that is really used, one which does not have the X-bar (the mean) in it. It is determined by simple algebra and is:

$$\sigma = \sqrt{[\Sigma(X^2) - (\Sigma X)^2/n]/n}.$$

These two standard deviation formulas are identical.

Once again, the sample formula (s) divides by n -1 because of the normal bias caused by small sample sizes. The formula is:

$$s = \sqrt{[\Sigma(X^2) - (\Sigma X)^2/n]/(n - 1)}.$$

Notice that, for this second formula, only three values need to be accumulated: the sum of the *X*'s squared, the sum of the *X*'s, and *n*. This is the form a computer uses.

Suppose the following 4 measurements are made: 2.12, 2.23, 2.50, 2.35. The standard deviation is:

$$s = \sqrt{[\Sigma(X^2) - (\Sigma X)^2/n]/(n - 1)} = \sqrt{[21.24 - (9.2)^2/4]/(4 - 1)} = 0.163.$$

Notice that the sample formula (using n -1) had to be used because the measurements form a sample and not the universe.

SHAPE CHARACTERISTICS

The normal curve is bell-shaped and symmetrical (see Figures 3.1, 3.2, and 3.3). Symmetrical means that when the curve is folded along its center, the left side will exactly match the right side — the two forms (left and right side forms) will be the same, and one will exactly cover the other.

The actual measurements are placed along the bottom or X-axis of a Cartesian coordinate system. The amount of each measurement (the number of times that particular measurement occurs) is measured by the height of the curve at that point (the Y-axis of a Cartesian coordinate graph). A normal curve can be thought of as representing a process, and the area under the curve can be thought of as containing 100% of all items produced on that process. The area below a particular number, or above a particular number, can be thought of as a percent of items that measure above or below that particular value. In this way, the curve also represents probability — the probability that any one item will measure below, or above, a particular value (the value used is usually an engineering specification, but it does not have to be).

Normal curves can be tall and narrow or low and flat, depending on the standard deviation (see Figure 3.2). There can be an infinite number of normal curves with the same shape but different centers (see Figure 3.1), and there can be an infinite number of normal curves with the same center but different shapes (see Figure 3.2). Therefore, there can be infinity squared number of normal curves (whatever that means), but in actual practice the number of normal curves is quite limited.

If a curve is not normal, it is usually skewed (having one tail longer than the other). Curves are considered to be positively skewed when the long tail is to the right, and negatively skewed when the long tail is to the left. This convention is also followed with *Z* scores. *Z* scores to the right are considered to be positive, while *Z* scores to the left are considered to be negative.

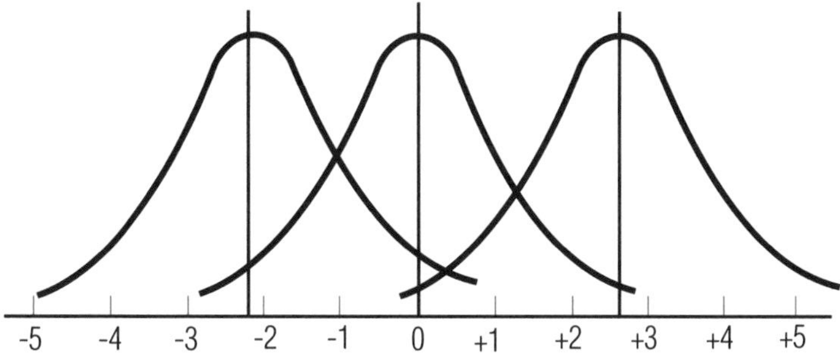

Figure 3.1. Normal curves with identical standard deviations but different means.

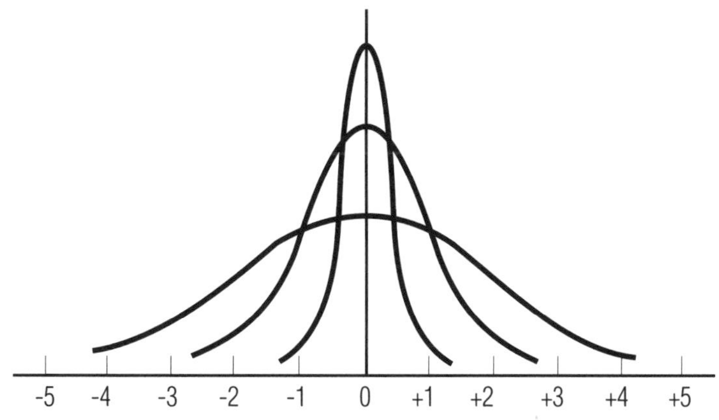

Figure 3.2. Normal curves with identical means but different standard deviations.

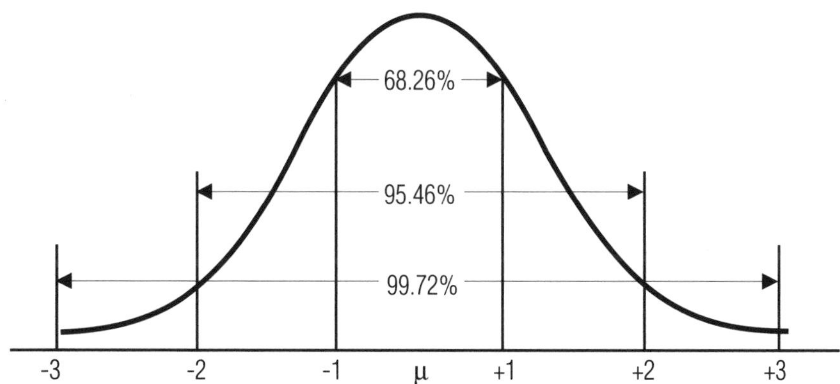

Figure 3.3. Percentage of items between 1, 2 and 3 standard deviations from the mean.

Z SCORES

The Z value is the number of standard deviations from the mean. It is found by the formula:

$$Z = (X - \mu)/\sigma$$

where Z is the number of standard deviations, X is a specification, μ (mu) is the mean of the universe distribution, and σ (sigma) is the universe standard deviation. What this formula really does is to transform the process normal curve into a standard normal curve with the mean equal to zero and the standard deviation equal to one (1.00...). In the process normal curve, the numbers along the bottom (X-axis) represent measurements, or observations. In the standard normal, these numbers represent standard deviations from the mean of zero (therefore positive to the right and negative to the left). If the sample is large enough (say, 100 or more, although some say that 30 or more is large enough) and unbiased, a sample formula can be used. The sample formula is the same as above except that μ is replaced with an X-bar, and σ is replaced with an s. The sample formula is:

$$Z = (X - \overline{X})/s.$$

(Control charts use a set of tables where the Z is already included.)

All normal curves have the same percent of area when compared to the number of standard deviations (the Z score). For instance, the percent of area between ±1 standard deviations (±1 σ) is always 68.26%. Note that this means that the percentage area under the curve from the mean to ±1 standard deviation (to the right of the mean) is always one-half of this, or 34.13%. The same is also true of -1 standard deviations (to the left of the mean). Between ±2 standard deviations (±2 σ), it is always 95.46%, and between ±3 standard deviations (±3 σ) it is always about 99.73% (see Figure 3.3). These percentages are shown as ratios (0.6826, 0.9546, and 0.9973) in the table of Z scores (Table 1, at the back of this book).

To use the Z tables (Table 1, at the back of this book), first calculate the Z value by using the Z formula above. Then find the Z value on the left side of the table and read the area in the body of the table (it may be necessary to interpolate). Also notice that the third digit in the Z score (the second after the period) occurs along the top of the table, not the side (thus, +1.25 can be found by locating +1.2 in the left column and then finding 0.05 at the top of the table and following it down until it intersects with the horizontal +1.2 row — the value is 0.8944). The value from the body of the table (the center) is a P value (a probability value). For practice, locate the following list of P values with their associated Z values in Table 1.

1. If $Z = +0.12$, $P = 0.5478$.
2. If $Z = +2.445$, $P = 0.9928$ (by interpolation).
3. If $Z = -1.05$, $P = 0.1469$.

Notice that the *P*'s are in ratios, not in percentages. This is the form that must be used in calculations. For instance, although the first *P* is 54.78%, it is the value in the table (0.5478) that must be used in all calculations. This value is often called the "area under the curve," because that is the area of the standard normal curve (as well as the percent of items, when multiplied by 100).

APPLICATIONS OF THE NORMAL CURVE

The normal curve can be used to determine a percent of items below a specified value, above a specified value, or between two specified values (these are the ones used by control charts). It can also be used to determine an upper limit, a lower limit, or a mean. These last three are used for other applications, and are called "inverse" applications of the normal.

Notice that the *Z* formula has several unknowns. When all but one are known, the unknown one can be calculated using simple algebra. This is the best way to determine these values (it is possible, of course, to determine a formula for each value, but then many formulas would be needed). Note how pictures simplify the thought processes and act as guides for solving the problem. With pictures, it is obvious what sign must be used, and almost obvious what percentage (approximately) will result.

Example 3.1

Find the percent of items below a certain value. The mean height of a certain product is 20 inches, with a standard deviation of 2 inches. Find the percent of items likely to be less than 16.5 inches.

$$Z = (16.5 - 20)/2 = -1.75$$
$$P(Z \leq -1.75) = 0.0401 \text{ or } 4.01\%.$$

This means that the probability that *Z* is less than or equal to -1.75 is 0.0401, or 4.01%. Therefore, the probability that any one part produced by the measured process will be under 16.5 inches is 4.01%, or 4.01% of all parts produced by the measured process will be under 16.5 inches (these are identical statements).

To illustrate this, first draw the normal curve (see Figure 3.4). Then locate all values on the drawing. Then calculate *Z* with the formula above and get the *P* value (0.0401) from the *Z* table. Now locate 0.0401 on the drawing and check to see if it is about correct by comparing the location on the curve to the percentages shown in Figure 3.3. (The numbers used here are estimated — in practice, they would almost always be calculated from actual measurements.)

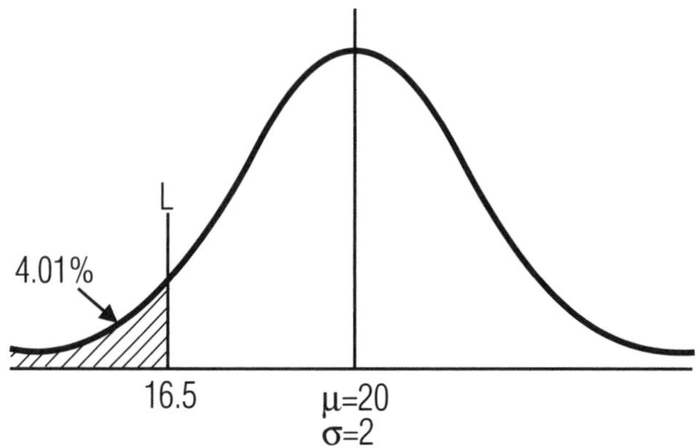

Figure 3.4. Curve illustrating Example 3.1.

Example 3.2

Find the percent of items above a certain value. The mean height of a certain product is 20 inches, with a standard deviation of 2 inches. Find the percent of items likely to be greater than 21.5 inches.

$$Z = (21.5 - 20)/2 = 0.75$$
$$P(Z > 0.75) = 1 - P(Z \leq 0.75) = 1 - 0.7734 = 0.2266 \text{ or } 22.66\%.$$

This means that the probability that Z is greater than 0.75 is equal to 1 minus the probability that Z is less than or equal to 0.75 (0.7734 from the Z table), which is equal to 0.2266 or 22.66%. Therefore, the probability that any one part produced by the measured process will be over 21.5 inches is 22.66%, or 22.66% of all parts produced by the measured process will be over 21.5 inches (these are identical statements).

To illustrate this example, draw the normal curve (see Figure 3.5). Then locate all values on the drawing. Then calculate Z and get the P value (0.7734) from the Z table. Then subtract 0.7734 from one (1.00...) to get 0.2266. Finally, locate 0.2266 on the drawing and check against Figure 3.3 to see if it is about correct.

Example 3.3

Find the percent of items between two values. The mean height of a certain product is 20 inches, with a standard deviation of 2 inches. Find the percent of items likely to be between 16.5 inches and 21.5 inches.

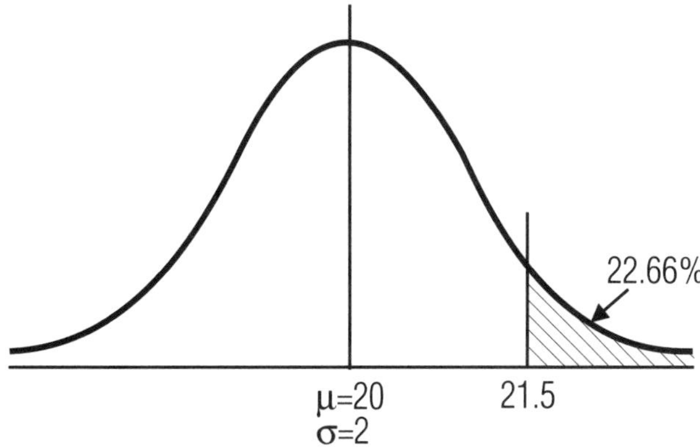

Figure 3.5. Curve illustrating Example 3.2.

$$P = 0.0401 \text{ and } 0.2266 \text{ (from Examples 3.1 and 3.2 above).}$$
$$P = 1 - (0.0401 + 0.2266) = 0.7333 \text{ or } 73.33\%.$$

This means that the probability that any one part produced by the measured process will be between 16.5 and 21.5 inches is 73.33%, or 73.33% of all parts produced by the measured process will be between 16.5 and 21.5 inches (these are identical statements).

To illustrate this, draw the normal curve (see Figure 3.6). Then locate all values on the drawing. Then determine the *P* values for each area. Then add the two *P* values and subtract from one. Then locate the *P* values on the drawing. Finally, check to see that the *P* values are about right. This answer can also be found by subtracting 0.0401 from 0.7734.

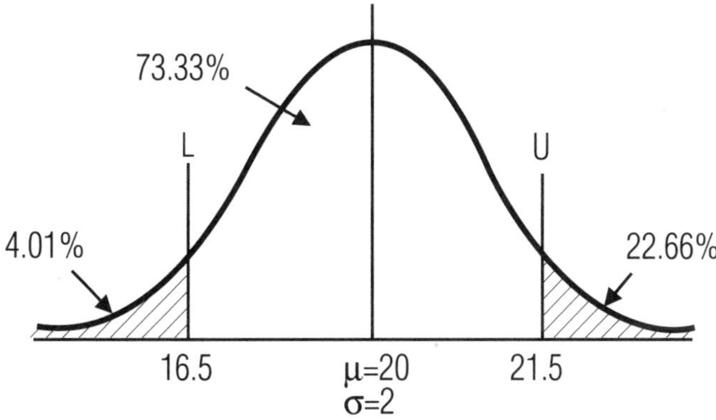

Figure 3.6. Curve illustrating Example 3.3.

CONTROL CHARTS AND THE NORMAL CURVE

The normal curve forms the theoretical foundation for all control charts. Variables charts use the normal curve direct, while attributes charts use the normal approximation to the binomial (p charts) and the normal approximation to the Poisson (u and c charts). However, all control charts use the normal curve theory.

Control charts are, essentially, just upended normal curves with the mean and ±3 standard deviation lines extended (see Chapter 7 for instructions on how to construct a normal curve). The centerline of the control chart closely approximates the mean of the normal, and the upper and lower limit lines of the control chart closely approximate the ±3 standard deviations of the normal. This is shown in Figure 3.7 (although the curve itself is never shown on the chart). If the mean and limits have been properly determined, and if the process is in control, then 99.73% of all items produced will fall within these limits. Since there is such a small probability (0.27%) that an in-control process will produce product outside the limits, it is assumed that product measuring outside the limits has been caused by a process problem. Therefore, a search is instituted to find the cause, and to correct it.

It is important, however, that the data plotted onto the control chart be normally distributed. Control charts (except the individuals chart) ensure this by the way the data (measurements) are collected, by the way the data are plotted (means of small samples rather than the individual measurements), and by the way the central value and chart limits are calculated.

However, the limit lines on the control chart are not specification limits. In fact, the control chart has nothing to do with specifications. It just shows what the process is capable of. Even if the specifications fall inside the control chart limits, bad parts can still be produced. Therefore, the specification limits must be compared with the control chart limits to see what the process can do with that product. See Chapter 6 for more explanation of this aspect of control charts.

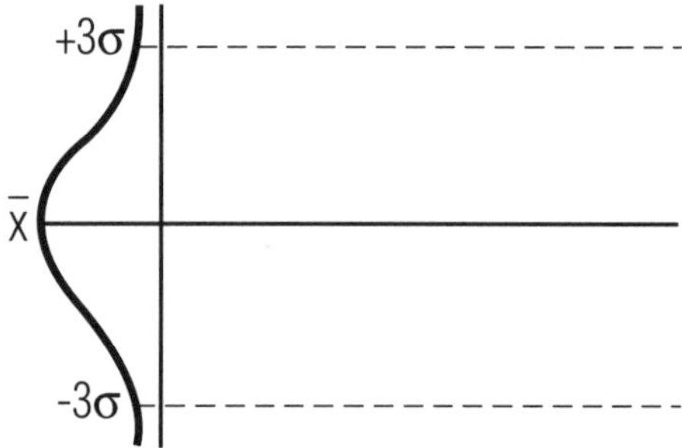

Figure 3.7. Curve illustrating the normal curve relationship to quality control charts.

— Chapter 4 —

VARIABLES CONTROL CHARTS

In quality control, the plotted points (*X*-bars) for variables charts are measured, while the plotted points for attributes charts (*p*'s, *u*'s, or *c*'s) are counted only (only the counting points of 1, 2, 3, etc., are used). Unlike attributes charts, variables charts can show a problem even before defectives are made. This is because patterns in the plotted points (which are almost always within the specifications when the process is in control) can be analyzed and point to possible problems before they get so big that defectives are made (see Chapter 6).

All variables charts (all of the charts in this chapter) come in two parts: an *X*-bar chart and an *R* chart (this is not true of attributes charts — they come in only one part). The means of small sample sizes are plotted on the *X*-bar chart and the ranges (dispersion) of these same sample sizes are plotted on the *R* chart (there is an *s*-bar chart which uses the standard deviations of each sample but it is not included here).

There are five variables charts shown here: the basic *X*-bar,*R*, zero-base coding, moving average, moving average using zero-base coding, and moving average using attributes data. The zero-base chart is probably the best chart available for short production runs. Although the moving average chart can be used for short production runs, it is best used for those situations where only one measurement at a time can be made. The moving average with zero-base is best when both of these situations are present, when there can be only one measurement at a time, *and* each production run is quite small. The moving average chart using attributes data can be used quite successfully for nonproductive and services activities (so can the basic moving average chart, when the data can be measured).

The difference between the mean and the limits is equal to 3σ (3 sigma, or 3 standard deviations). Therefore, if that difference is divided by 3 the result is 1σ. This is true of all control charts except some at the lower limit. *R* charts and attributes charts are all truncated at zero when the calculations come out to a minus number (for small sample sizes, mostly). This is important when analyzing chart patterns (see Chapter 6).

In order to use a variables chart, the critical characteristic must be measured. If it cannot be measured, then the moving average chart using attributes data must be used (or one of the attributes charts from Chapter 5). Sometimes a characteristic can be measured, but it is still best to use an attributes chart. For instance, an electric harness may have a measurable length characteristic with a specification of ± 1 or 2 inches. However, the line is placed around and through other parts so that having a perfect length (close to the midpoint) has no meaning. In this case, an attributes chart is perfectly adequate.

For variables control charts, a constant subgroup size is assumed (always measure the next 4 consecutive units produced, for instance) even though it is possible to vary the subgroup sizes (4 one time, 6 the next, 4 the next, 8 the next, etc.). The reasons for this are threefold. First, variable subgroup sizes require the calculation of control limits for each subgroup and are quite difficult to use, leading to an increased likelihood of errors. More important, however, is the fact that variable subgroup size chart limits cannot be determined ahead of time, thus destroying the predictive nature of the chart. Finally, for variables charts, the nature of the situation is such that there is almost never a time when a constant subgroup cannot be used, so that the difficulties inherent in variable subsampling need never be confronted. This is not true, however, for many attributes charts because of the large sample sizes required.

It is important to understand that the control chart plots are averages of small samples. Therefore, any one of the small sample measurements can be outside the control chart limits without the average being out. The chart controls on averages only, not on individual measurements. Any individual measurements that fall outside of the control limits are ignored (unless they also fall outside the specifications limits, in which case they are nonconformances). In Figure 4.1, sample #4 has an individual measurement that is outside of the chart control limits. However, this measurement is ignored because the average is not outside. Sample #6, however, is outside the limits because its average is outside. An investigation would be launched to find out why the four measurements of sample #6 are so far above the upper limit. However, the one high value in sample #4 is not investigated (because its average is within the limits).

It is recommended for all the variables charts shown here (and for all control charts, actually) that the start-up number of subgroups be 25. The subgroup size will vary according to the kind of chart used. The formulas for each of the following variables charts will be explained and illustrated in conjunction with a practical example.

THE BASIC *X*-BAR, *R* CONTROL CHART

This is the most basic, and most used, of all variables charts. It actually forms the model for all control charts. It is used for ongoing long-run products where sample cost is high and the risk of sample error is low. Periodic random samples (subgroups) are taken of successive units produced (it is best to use 4 at a time in succession), and the subgroup samples are taken at random times of the day. It is recommended that this chart use a subgroup size of 4 with 25 subgroups for the initial, start-up sample size (although the subgroup size can go much higher — see Table 2 at the end of the book).

$\overline{\overline{X}}$ in the formulas is equivalent to the mean of the normal curve (the μ of Chapter 2). $A_2\overline{R}$ is equivalent to 3 standard deviations (the σ of Chapter 2) from the mean. Therefore, the area between the limits is equal to 0.9973, or there is a 99.73% probability that any one sample average, from a process in control, will fall between the limits.

Example 4.1.

Use the data in Figure 4.1 to construct an $\overline{X}$,*R* chart. Use a subgroup size of four, as the chart shows.

$$\Sigma\overline{X}\text{ (for 25 subgroups)} = 26.47, \text{ and } \Sigma R = 0.241.$$

Solution:

1. Collect the samples (subgroups), enter them onto the chart, and calculate the subgroup averages and ranges. This has already been done in Figure 4.1 for the first six plots. The following calculation of the first subgroup average and range will be used as an example of these calculations.

$$\overline{X}_1 = \Sigma X/n = (1.061 + 1.062 + 1.066 + 1.053)/4 = 1.0605$$

$$R_1 = X_H - X_L = 1.066 - 1.053 = 0.013.$$

2. Calculate limits and midpoints for both $\overline{X}$ and R charts. m = the number of subgroups; and A_2, D_3, and D_4 are values from Table 2 at the end of the book.

   $\overline{\overline{X}} = \Sigma X/m = 26.47/25 = 1.0588$

   $\overline{R} = \Sigma R/m = 0.241/25 = 0.00964$

   $UCL_{X\text{-}Bar} = \overline{\overline{X}} + A_2\overline{R} = 1.0588 + 0.729(0.00964) = 1.0658$

L.A.Doty Co. Page ____ of _____

X-BAR,R CONTROL CHART

PART NO.: _________ PART NAME: ________________________ SPEC: __________

OPERATOR(S): ____________________ INSPECTOR(S): ________________________

PROCESS: ____________________________________ CHART NO: ____________

GAGES: ______________________________________ DATE: ____/____/____

$UCL_{\overline{X}}$ = 1.0658

$\overline{X}$ = 1.0588

$LCL_{\overline{X}}$ = 1.0518

UCL_R = 0.022

$\overline{R}$ = 0.00964

LCL_R = 0.000

X_1	1.061	1.064	1.067	1.062	1.055	1.081
X_2	1.062	1.065	1.066	1.071	1.052	1.089
X_3	1.066	1.063	1.059	1.070	1.066	1.079
X_4	1.053	1.061	1.063	1.057	1.059	1.077
X-BAR	1.0605	1.0633	1.0638	1.0650	1.0580	1.0815
RANGE	0.013	0.004	0.008	0.010	0.014	0.012
DATE	3/1	3/1	3/2	3/2	3/2	3/5
TIME	8:06	10:35	2:00	3:15	4:20	9:55

Figure 4.1. Sample *X*-bar, *R* control chart.

$$LCL_{X\text{-}Bar} = \overline{\overline{X}} - A_2\overline{R} = 1.0588 - 0.729(0.00964) = 1.0518$$
$$UCL_R = D_4\overline{R} = 2.282(0.00964) = 0.022$$
$$LCL_R = D_3\overline{R} = 0(0.00964) = 0.000.$$

3. Construct the control chart and plot the values (all X-bars and R's, even those that are outside the limits). Figure 4.1 shows a portion of the chart as designed for actual use, with measurements and calculations entered onto the chart. The real chart would be large enough for all 25, or more, subgroups (probably more because it should contain a whole month's worth of data).
4. Display the chart in a conspicuous place and continue to measure and plot. Also continue to recalculate monthly. It is best for the operator to do the measuring and plotting, and to control the process. (See Chapter 6 for a discussion of chart analysis.)

THE *X*-BAR,*R* CHART USING ZERO-BASE CODING

The coding procedure of this chart makes it possible to chart more than one product on the same chart (remember that control charts control the process, not the product). This is one of the few variables charts where this is possible. This makes it an excellent chart to use for short production runs — probably the best one.

This chart is identical to the basic X-bar,R chart except that all measurements are coded, and the plotted values — the averages (X-bars) and ranges (R's) — are calculated from these coded values. The coded values represent distances from the respective specification midpoints rather than the actual measurements, which is why many similar products can be charted on the same chart (the coding puts them all on the same footing, as far as charting is concerned).

There are several requirements as follows.

1. The products must be similar.
2. The plotted characteristics must be identical (although the engineering specifications do not need to be). Each chart is for one characteristic on one process. Actually, it is possible to chart any number of different processes on this chart, as well as products, but the chart would then lose its ability to provide information for problem correction and process improvement. Without this ability, any chart is essentially worthless (see Chapter 6).
3. Only variables data can be used.

4. The materials must be similar. Two different types of metals, for instance, would probably have different causes for any one nonconformance problem.
5. Although they do not have to be exact, the ranges must be similar (although similar products on the same process should almost guarantee this condition).

The coding formula is:

coded value = measurement - specification midpoint.

The specification in the formula refers to the engineering specification for the particular product characteristic being measured, so the specification midpoint is almost certain to be different for most products being charted.

Once the coded values are determined, the remainder of the procedures and formulas are identical to those of the basic *X*-bar,*R* chart.

Example 4.2.

Construct a zero-base *X*-bar,*R* chart using the data from Figure 4.2, and using the specification midpoint as the zero base. Plot the coded values on the revised charts. $\Sigma\overline{X}$ (for 25 subgroups) = 0.021, and $\Sigma R = 0.4125$.

Solution:

1. Collect the samples (subgroups) and code each one. Then enter them onto the chart and calculate the subgroup averages and ranges. This has already been done in Figure 4.2 for the first six plots. The following calculation of the first subgroup average and range will be used as an example of these calculations.

   Coded $\overline{X}_1$ = measurement - specification midpoint = 1.534 - 1.5425 = -0.0085

   $X_1 = \Sigma X/n = (-0.0085 + 0.0025 + -0.0065 + 0.0035)/4 = -0.0023$

   $R_1 = X_H - X_L = 0.0035 - -0.0085 = 0.012.$

2. Calculate the limits and midpoint for both X and R. m = the number of subgroups; and A_2, D_3, and D_4 are values from Table 2 at the end of the book.

   $\overline{\overline{X}} = \Sigma\overline{X}/m = 0.021/25 = 0.00084$

   $\overline{R} = \Sigma R/m = 0.4125/25 = 0.0165$

   $UCL_{X\text{-}Bar} = \overline{\overline{X}} + A_2\overline{R} = 0.00084 + 0.729(0.0165) = 0.013$

   $LCL_{X\text{-}Bar} = \overline{\overline{X}} - A_2\overline{R} = 0.00084 - 0.729(0.0165) = -0.011$

   $UCL_R = D_4\overline{R} = 2.282(0.0165) = 0.038$

   $LCL_R = D_3\overline{R} = 0(0.0165) = 0.$

3. Construct the control chart and plot the values (all X-bars and R's, even those that are outside the limits). Figure 4.2 shows a portion of the chart as designed for actual use, with measurements and calcula-

L.A.Doty Co. Page ____ of ____

X-BAR,R CONTROL CHART USING CODED DATA

PART NO.: ________ PART NAME: ________________ SPEC: ________

OPERATOR(S): ____________ INSPECTOR(S): ____________

PROCESS: ____________________ CHART NO: ________

GAGES: ____________________ DATE: ____/____/____

$UCL_{\bar{X}} = 0.013$

$\bar{\bar{X}} = 0.00084$

$LCL_{\bar{X}} = 0.011$

$UCL_R = 0.038$

$\bar{R} = 0.0165$

$LCL_R = 0.000$

X_1	-0.0085	0.006	-0.0055	-0.011	0.005	0.004
X_2	0.0025	0.007	0.0045	0.005	-0.009	-0.001
X_3	-0.0065	-0.001	0.0105	-0.000	-0.013	-0.002
X_4	0.0035	-0.000	-0.0125	0.003	0.009	-0.001
X-BAR	-0.0023	0.0030	-0.0008	-0.0008	-0.0020	0.0000
RANGE	0.012	0.008	0.035	0.016	0.022	0.006
DATE/TIME						
PRODUCT	A	B	C	D	E	E
MIDPOINT	1.5425	1.643	1.5895	1.876	1.582	1.885

Figure 4.2. Sample *X*-bar,*R* control chart using coded data.

tions entered onto the chart. The real chart would be large enough for all 25, or more, subgroups (probably more because it should contain a whole month's worth of data).

4. Display the chart in a conspicuous place and continue to measure and plot. Also continue to recalculate monthly. It is best for the operator to do the measuring and plotting, and to control the process.

THE MOVING AVERAGE/MOVING RANGE CHART

With this chart, the measurements are collected individually (one measurement every so often instead of 4 at a time, for instance), *X*-bars are determined by using a moving average of three (average the first three; then 2, 3, and 4; then 3, 4, and 5, etc.), and the range is determined by subtracting the low from the high of each of these sets of three. The subgroup size is always 3; larger subgroup sizes smooth out the variation too much. In start up, the first 2 measurements are not charted (because no average or range is available) so that there are always two less plotted values than the number of measurements (23 plotted values for 25 measurements).

One problem with this procedure is that it uses much less than the usual 100 or more measurements to start the chart. Even so, it still essentially maintains normality, mainly because of the moving average procedure, and because the normal curve is "robust" in this situation (fairly large deviations from normal will not materially affect the outcome).

Although this chart can be used for short production runs and/or long process times, it is especially useful for processes where it is not practical to take successive samples, such as chemical processes and processes where very little variation occurs from piece to piece so that more time and units are needed for a significant variation to accumulate (such as in bottling plants).

Example 4.3.

Construct an *X*-bar,*R* chart using the moving average procedure and using the data from Figure 4.3.

$$\Sigma X \text{ (for the first 25 subgroups)} = 24.376, \text{ and } \Sigma R = 0.198.$$

Solution:

1. Collect the samples (in this case, the samples are individual measurements), enter them onto the chart, and calculate the subgroup averages and ranges. This has already been done in Figure 4.3 for the first six measurements. The following calculation of the first two

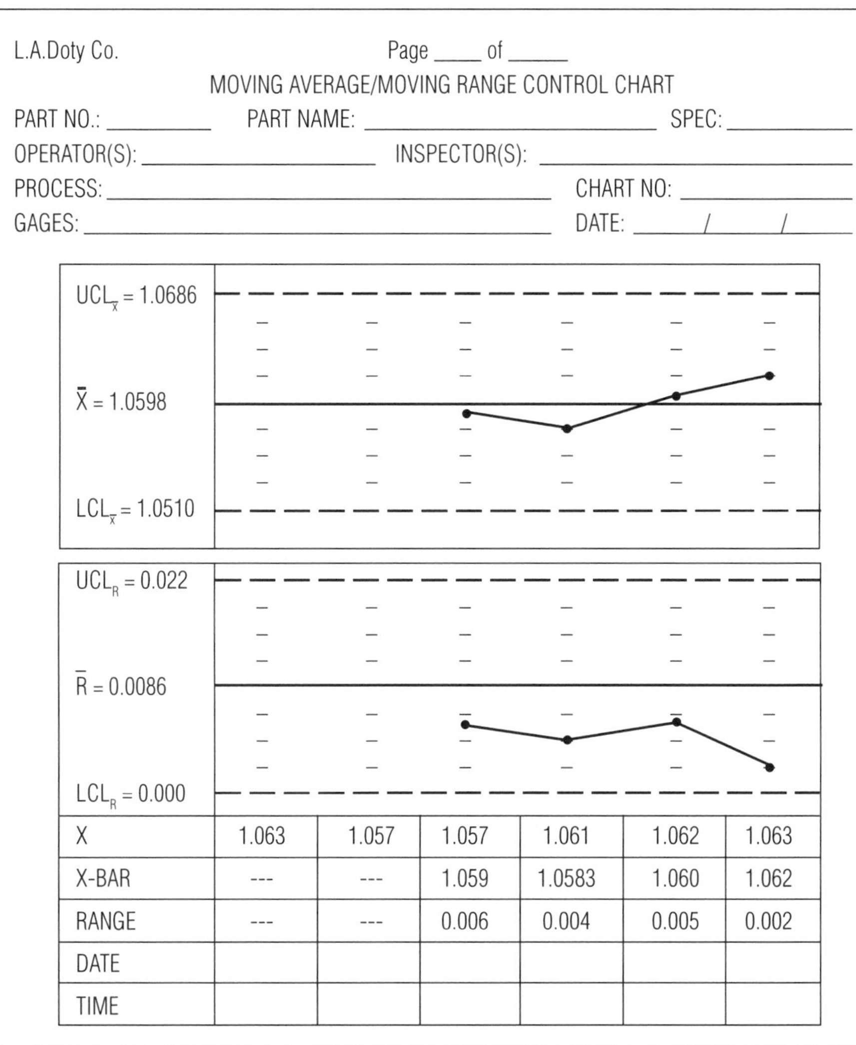

L.A.Doty Co. Page ____ of ____

MOVING AVERAGE/MOVING RANGE CONTROL CHART

PART NO.: ________ PART NAME: ____________ SPEC: ________

OPERATOR(S): ____________ INSPECTOR(S): ____________

PROCESS: ____________ CHART NO: ________

GAGES: ____________ DATE: ___/___/___

$UCL_{\bar{X}} = 1.0686$

$\bar{X} = 1.0598$

$LCL_{\bar{X}} = 1.0510$

$UCL_R = 0.022$

$\bar{R} = 0.0086$

$LCL_R = 0.000$

X	1.063	1.057	1.057	1.061	1.062	1.063
X-BAR	---	---	1.059	1.0583	1.060	1.062
RANGE	---	---	0.006	0.004	0.005	0.002
DATE						
TIME						

Figure 4.3. Partial moving average control chart.

subgroup averages and ranges (for measurements 3 and 4) will be used as an example of these calculations. Note that there are no *X*-bars or *R*'s at measurements 1 and 2. This occurs only on the first (or start-up) chart, and only because there are no earlier measurements with which to average. The calculations of the first two *X*-bars and *R*'s are:

$$\overline{X_3} = \Sigma X/n = (1.063 + 1.057 + 1.057)/3 = 1.059$$

$$R_3 = X_H - X_L = 1.063 - 1.057 = 0.006$$

$\overline{X}_4 = \Sigma X/n = (1.057 + 1.057 + 1.061)/3 = 1.0583$

$R_4 = X_H - X_L = 1.061 - 1.057 = 0.004.$

2. Calculate the chart midpoints and limits. Once the moving averages and ranges are determined, the remaining chart procedures and formulas are identical to those of the basic *X*-bar,*R* charts. Note that the conversion factors from Table 2 at the end of the book (for a sample of 3) have been entered into the formulas as constants (1.023 for A_2, 2.575 for D_4, and 0 for D_3). This is because the subgroup size never changes — it is always 3.

   $\overline{\overline{X}} = \Sigma\overline{X}/(m - 2) = 24.376/(25 - 2) = 1.0598$

   $\overline{R} = \Sigma R/(m - 2) = 0.198/(25 - 2) = 0.0086$

   $UCL_X = \overline{\overline{X}} + 1.023\overline{R} = 1.0598 + 1.023(0.0086) = 1.0686$

   $LCL_X = \overline{\overline{X}} - 1.023\overline{R} = 1.0598 - 1.023(0.0086) = 1.0510$

   $UCL_R = 2.575\overline{R} = 2.575(0.0086) = 0.022$

   $LCL_R = = 0.000.$

3. Construct the control chart and plot the values (all *X*-bars and *R*'s, even those that are outside the limits). Figure 4.3 shows a portion of the chart as designed for actual use, with measurements and calculations entered onto the chart. The real chart would be large enough for all 25, or more, subgroups (probably more because it should contain a whole month's worth of data).
4. Display the chart in a conspicuous place and continue to measure and plot. Also continue to recalculate monthly. It is best for the operator to do the measuring and plotting, and to control the process.

THE MOVING AVERAGE CONTROL CHART USING ZERO-BASE CODING

This chart is identical to the basic moving average chart except that the measurements are coded prior to plotting, as was done for the *X*-bar,*R* chart using zero-base coding. The coding procedures and formula are identical to those of that other zero-base coding chart.

$$\text{Coded value} = \text{measurement} - \text{specification midpoint.}$$

Once the coded values are determined, the chart construction and use proceeds as in the basic moving average chart.

The moving average with zero-base is best when there can be only one measurement at a time *and* each production run is quite small.

Example 4.4.

Determine the control chart for the coded data of Figure 4.4. Notice that there are no X-bars or R's for the first two X's (measurements, or observations). Also notice that the X-bars and R's for the first measurement of product B (sixth X; sixth measurement; sixth subgroup) are derived using the last two measurements from the previous product (product A). This is possible only if the two products are produced one after the other. If another product is produced between them, and not charted, then a new chart must be started.

$$\Sigma X \text{ (for the first 25 subgroups)} = -0.0031, \text{ and } \Sigma R = 0.1418.$$

Solution:

1. Collect the measurements, code them, and enter them onto the chart. Then calculate the subgroup averages (X-bars) and the subgroup ranges (R's) and total. This has already been done in Figure 4.4 for the first six measurements. Averages and ranges for subgroups 3, 4, and 6 are shown below as examples.

   $\overline{X}_3 = \Sigma X/n = (-\,0.0015 + -\,0.0055 + 0.0035)/3 = -0.0012$
   $\overline{X}_4 = \Sigma X/n = (-\,0.0055 + 0.0035 + 0.0005)/3 = -0.0005$
   $\overline{X}_6 = \Sigma X/n = (0.0005 + 0.0005 + 0.0000)/3 = 0.0003$
   $R_3 = X_H - X_L = (0.0035 - -0.0055) = 0.0090$
   $R_4 = X_H - X_L = (0.0035 - -0.0055) = 0.0090$
   $R_6 = X_H - X_L = (0.0005 - 0.0000) = 0.0005.$

2. Calculate the midpoints and limits. Note that the conversion factors taken from Table 2 at the back of the book (for a sample of 3) have been entered into the formulas as constants (1.023 for A_2, 2.575 for D_4, and 0 for D_3). This is because the subgroup size never changes — it is always 3.

   $\overline{\overline{X}} = \Sigma\overline{X}/(m - 2) = -0.0031/(25 - 2) = -0.000135$
   $R = \Sigma R/(m - 2) = 0.1418/(25 - 2) = 0.0062$
   $UCL_{X\text{-}Bar} = \overline{\overline{X}} + 1.023\overline{R} = -\,0.000135 + 1.023(0.0062) = 0.0062$
   $LCL_{X\text{-}Bar} = \overline{\overline{X}} - 1.023\overline{R} = -\,0.000135 - 1.023(0.0062) = -0.0065$
   $UCL_R = 2.575\overline{R} = 2.575(0.0062) = 0.0160$
   $LCL_R = 0.$

L.A.Doty Co. Page ____ of ____

ZERO-BASE/MOVING RANGE CONTROL CHART

PART NO.: ________ PART NAME: ____________ SPEC: ________

OPERATOR(S): ____________ INSPECTOR(S): ____________

PROCESS: ____________ CHART NO: ________

GAGES: ____________ DATE: ___/___/___

$UCL_{\bar{X}} = 0.0062$

$\bar{\bar{X}} = 0.000135$

$LCL_{\bar{X}} = 0.0065$

$UCL_R = 0.0160$

$\bar{R} = 0.0062$

$LCL_R = 0.000$

SUBSAMPLE PRODUCT DATE TIME	1 A	2 A	3 A	4 A	5 A	6 B
USL MID LSL	1.344 1.3375 1.331					1.446 1.438 1.430
MEASURE	1.336	1.332	1.341	1.338	1.338	1.438
CODED	-0.0015	-0.0055	0.0035	0.0005	0.0005	0.0000
X-bar	—	—	-0.0012	-0.0005	0.0015	0.0003
R	—	—	0.009	0.009	0.003	0.0005

Figure 4.4. Partial moving average chart using zero-base coding.

3. Construct the control chart and plot the values (all *X*-bars and *R*'s, even those that are outside the limits). Figure 4.4 shows a portion of the chart as designed for actual use, with measurements and calculations entered onto the chart. The real chart would be large enough for all 25, or more, subgroups (probably more because it should contain a whole month's worth of data).

4. Display the chart in a conspicuous place and continue to measure and plot. Also continue to recalculate monthly. It is best for the operator to do the measuring and plotting, and to control the process.

THE MOVING AVERAGE CHART USING ATTRIBUTES DATA

In general, attributes data should not be used for variables charts, unless necessary. The reason for this is the necessary "judgment" that must be employed, and the near impossibility of getting everyone to "judge" the same way. Therefore, when attributes data are converted into variables data, a great deal of judgmental variation is usually created, as well as the normal process variation. This "judgmental variation" is, of course, extremely undesirable. Nevertheless, there are a few circumstances when this type of chart can be profitably used, mostly in conjunction with nonmanufacturing processes.

Attributes data can be used, when converted into variables data, with either the basic X-bar,R chart or the moving average chart. However, the nature of attributes data is such that the moving average chart is almost always preferable since it is often impossible to obtain 4 or more measurements that follow each other, as in the basic X-bar,R chart (especially with nonmanufacturing processes). Therefore, the moving average chart shall be used to illustrate the technique. Actually, the only difference in using either chart is in the conversion procedure, after which the chart construction and use continues as already explained for either the basic X-bar,R chart or the moving average chart.

The best method of converting attributes data into variables data is to use a weighting procedure and assess the value of the observation on a predetermined scale (such as a scale of 1 to 5, 1 to 10, etc.). It is vitally important, with this method, that each weight be completely described, and that all evaluators be thoroughly trained in what the descriptions mean. It is best to use a team, and a team average, if possible, to smooth and reduce the "judgmental" variations (a team is best, for instance, on cosmetic characteristics or on measures that persist over time). However, it is often impossible to use a team, as in the example that follows.

The moving average chart using attributes data, as well as the basic moving average chart, can be used quite successfully for nonproductive and service activities. However, the moving average chart must have a measurement, while the moving average with attributes data does not, it needs instead a judgment as to the degree of quality.

Example 4.5.

Use the attributes data from Figure 4.5 to construct a moving average chart.

$$\Sigma\overline{X} \text{ (for the first 25 subgroups)} = 161.3, \text{ and } \Sigma R = 126.$$

Solution:

As each error was observed, the analyst made an instant assessment of degree of nonconformance (weighting) on a scale of 1 to 20, and recorded the weighting as well as the error and time of error (time is often important in later analysis and corrective activities). Even though there are not quite enough data (22 observations instead of 25) for a completely viable (statistically viable) chart, they must still be used in order to analyze the process. Any conclusions reached from this chart, therefore, must be carefully examined before application. This is often the case with this type of data, emphasizing again the need for care in the use of these charts.

Once the weighted values are determined, the chart construction proceeds exactly as it does for the basic moving average chart. Figure 4.5 shows a partial chart of the example. The calculations are as follows.

1. Collect the data, code (judge the degree of quality), and enter onto the control chart. Then calculate the means and the ranges. This has already been done in Figure 4.5 for the first six coded values. Subgroups 3 and 4 are presented as examples of the calculation procedures. The first two subgroups, of course, are not shown because this is a start-up chart, and there are no prior measurements.

   $\overline{X}_3 = \Sigma X/3 = (4 + 10 + 4)/3 = 6.0$

   $R_3 = X_H - X_L = 10 - 4 = 6$

   $\overline{X}_4 = \Sigma X/3 = (10 + 4 + 6)/3 = 6.7$

   $R_4 = X_H - X_L = 10 - 4 = 6.$

2. Calculate the midpoints and limits. Note that the conversion factors taken from Table 2 at the back of the book (for a sample of 3) have been entered into the formulas as constants (1.023 for A_2, 2.575 for D_4, and 0 for D_3). This is because the subgroup size never changes — it is always 3.

   $\overline{\overline{X}} = \Sigma\overline{X}/(m - 2) = 161.3/(22 - 2) = 8.065$

   $\overline{R} = \Sigma R/(m - 2) = 126/(22 - 2) = 6.3$

   $UCL_{X\text{-}Bar} = \overline{\overline{X}} + 1.023\overline{R} = 7.013 + 1.023(5.478) = 12.617$

   $LCL_{X\text{-}Bar} = \overline{\overline{X}} - 1.023\overline{R} = 7.013 - 1.023(5.478) = 1.409$

$$UCL_R = 2.575\overline{R} = 2.575(5.478) = 14.106$$
$$LCL_R = 0.$$

3. Construct the control chart and plot the values (all X-bars and R's, even those that are outside the limits). Figure 4.5 shows a portion of the chart as designed for actual use, with measurements and calculations entered onto the chart. The real chart would be large enough for all 25, or more, subgroups (probably more because it should contain a whole month's worth of data).

L.A.Doty Co. Page ____ of ____

MOVING AVERAGE/MOVING RANGE CONTROL CHART

PART NO.: ________ PART NAME: ____________________ SPEC: ________

OPERATOR(S): ______________ INSPECTOR(S): ______________

PROCESS: ____________________ CHART NO: ________

GAGES: ____________________ DATE: ___/___/___

$UCL_{\overline{X}} = 14.51$

$\overline{\overline{X}} = 8.065$

$LCL_{\overline{X}} = 1.62$

$UCL_R = 16.22$

$\overline{R} = 6.3$

$LCL_R = 0.0$

X	4	10	4	6	11	8
X-BAR	- - -	- - -	6.0	6.7	7.0	8.3
RANGE	- - -	- - -	6	6	7	5
DATE	3/1	3/1	3/2	3/2	3/2	3/5
TIME	8:06	10:35	2:00	3:15	4:20	9:55

Figure 4.5. Partial moving average control chart using attributes data.

4. Display the chart in a conspicuous place and continue to measure and plot. Also continue to recalculate monthly. It is best for the operator to do the measuring and plotting, and to control the process.

OTHER VARIABLES CHARTS

The *X*-bar,*s* chart is identical to the *X*-bar,*R* chart except that the standard deviation is used instead of the range, and samples of 10 or more are used instead of 4 (the size will usually depend on sampling cost and the cost of sampling error, and will frequently be determined by management and/or engineering).

The trend chart has upward, or downward, sloping centerline and limits, which must be calculated using fairly complicated regression formulas. The reason for the sloping lines is to account for wear on tools. For this reason, it is often called the tool chart, and is used to determine when to replace worn-out tools.

The pre-control chart, also called the stoplight chart, is used to control production when the operator has a great deal of control. It is good for control of production and can be started immediately. However, it cannot be used for pattern analysis (as explained in Chapter 6).

The individuals chart is used when products take a very long time to complete (weeks, usually) and there is no way that more than one measurement can be made at a time (and more than one measurement would be meaningless due to the nature of the process). It is also necessary that this type of chart be used only on a process where normally distributed data are being produced. Other charts ensure normality by the way the data are collected and used (averages and ranges of small sample sizes), but this one does not.

The specifications chart uses specifications as the limit lines, and can, therefore, be started immediately. However, if the process is off center from the specification center, the chart can give erroneous information (such as entries outside of the limits when they are really not, and entries inside the limits when they should be outside).

Run charts are not statistical charts at all. They are just plots of each individual measurement (or sometimes of each small sample average). These charts are almost always used as a check on the process prior to the installation of a statistical chart.

Constant limit charts plot the number of average deviations from the mean, rather than the average measurements (using a complicated formula for each plot). The limits are constants, and more than one product can be charted at one time (as in the zero-base charts). However, the calculations are complicated, there is no way to calculate C_p ratios, and the chart limits do not show process improvements. For a further explanation of the above charts, see Doty, 1996.

Multivariate charts are used to control two or more interrelated characteristics at one time, on the same chart. The calculations are very complicated, and the chart has very limited use (see Montgomery, 1985, p. 245).

— Chapter 5 —

ATTRIBUTES CONTROL CHARTS

In quality control, the plotted points for attributes charts (p's, u's, or c's) are counted only — that is, only the counting numbers of 1, 2, 3, etc., are used. These counted data (plotted points), if non-zero, are always outside the specification limits — they always represent defectives (the unit on which a defect occurs is always a defective). Therefore, non-zero attributes data, even though falling within the chart's control limits, should always be examined for ways of eliminating the problems that cause them.

All attributes charts should have a place for types of defects (a kind of automatic Pareto chart, see Chapter 7) so that the analyst can know which type of defect, and its causes, to first examine (in a Pareto analysis, the highest percentage should be analyzed first). For instance, in Figure 5.1 the greatest number of defects is undersized units. Therefore, the analyst should first investigate the causes of undersized units and try to eliminate them.

As with variables charts, the start-up sample size for attributes charts should be 25 subgroups. The subgroup size, however, must be determined from the process average. If the subgroup size is too large, unnecessary cost is incurred. If too small, too many subgroups of zero defectives will occur, destroying the predictive nature of the chart. Therefore, some pre-knowledge of the process average is needed to know what the subgroup size must be. If this pre-knowledge is not available, the subgroup size must be estimated. For example, suppose that a process normally runs about 1% defective, or that a pre-chart sample showed a probable 1% defective rate, or that a similar product run on the same process has a 1% defective rate, or that engineering management has determined that the process will run about 1% defective for this product. A subgroup size of 100 would, then, have an average of 1 defective for each subgroup (one outside the specification limits). However, some of these subgroups would have many defectives while some would have none at all, with a large probability that a very large percentage of the first 25 subgroups would have zero defectives. Because of this, charts constructed from these subgroups would be useless. In this case, a subgroup size of about 500 would be needed ($n = 5/p$-bar $= 5/0.01 = 500$). The same logic is true also of u charts, although the same n formula is not used.

Also, as the process is perfected, the process average tends to decrease, which means that the subgroup size must then be increased. Ongoing, steady-state, attributes charts tend to have fairly large subgroup sizes. Subgroup sizes of 300 to 3,000 are common for p charts, and 20 to 100 for u charts (c charts always have a subgroup size of 1).

As with R charts, when the lower control limit (LCL) of an attributes chart calculates to a negative number, it is changed to zero (there cannot be a negative number of defectives or defects).

The formulas for the following attributes charts will be explained and illustrated in conjunction with practical examples. Notice that all attributes charts have a column for the chart totals. For the start-up chart, these totals would be for the start-up size of 25 subgroups. All subsequent charts totals would be for an entire month.

CONSTANT SAMPLE SIZE *p* CHART (The Basic *p* Chart)

This chart controls on defective units (p), not defects per unit (u or c). The plotted value is the fraction defective (p), determined by dividing the number of defective units in the subgroup by the total number of units in the subgroup. Because of the way p is measured (part of the whole divided by the whole) it is also a probability value — the probability that any one unit in the subgroup is defective.

To be effective in control charts, p must be smaller than 0.15 (or 15%). The normal curve approximation that makes the p chart work (makes it theoretically correct) does not apply to p values greater than 0.15. However, as far as quality control is concerned, this is no problem because p values greater than 0.15 (15%) indicate a process so far out of control that it should not need a control chart to show it (it should be obvious just from observing the process).

An excellent way of determining the appropriate subgroup size for a p chart is by using the following formula:

$$n = 5/p\text{-bar}$$

where n is the subgroup size (for a variable subgroup size chart, the average subgroup size should be used). The p-bar ($\overline{p}$) can be the p-bar from other, similar, products run on the same process (called the process average), or a $\overline{p}$ calculated from a sample run prior to charting, or even an informed estimate of the process average.

In almost all p chart applications, percentages are used on the chart instead of the fraction defective (in this form it is called the 100p chart). The reason for this is that most people are much more comfortable with percentages than with fractions or decimals. Only the final values (central value, limits, and plotted p's) are actually changed to percentages (multiplied by 100). Of course, percentages are never used in the actual calculations. All p charts used in this text follow this convention.

Note that when the lower control limit (LCL) calculates to a negative number, it is changed to zero (there cannot be a negative number of defectives).

The p-bar in the limit formulas approximates the μ (mu) or midpoint of the normal distribution. And $\sqrt{[\overline{p}(1-\overline{p})/n]}$ approximates the standard deviation (σ or sigma) of the normal distribution. The 3 in the formulas refers to 3 standard deviations from the mean.

Example 5.1.

Construct a p chart using the data from Figure 5.1. Note that all of the data are not there —only the first seven p's and the totals. However, this is enough to construct the chart. Also note that the total number of defects is more than the total number of defectives. This is almost always true. There can be more than one defect on a defective. It's the defects that cause the defective units. The reason for showing the number and type of defects is that this provides information for solving problems. It also provides an almost automatic Pareto analysis so that the analyst can know what kind of defects cause the most problems. Remember that all non-zero attributes plots represent a percentage of defectives. Since the cause of all defectives should be eliminated, all non-zero attributes plots should be investigated, if possible (even if they are not outside of the upper limit).

Solution:

1. Collect the samples (subgroups), enter them onto the chart, and calculate the subgroup averages. This has already been done in Figure

5.1 for the first seven plots. The following calculation of the first subgroup average will be used as an example of these calculations.

$p_1 = np/n = 15/500 = 0.030$ (or 3.0%).

2. Calculate the control limits and central value. *np* is the number of defective units in the subgroup. *p* is the percent average (actually ratio) for that subgroup. $\overline{p}$ (*p*-bar) is the average per subgroup for the start-up sample. $n\overline{p}$ (*np*-bar) is the average number of defective units in the start-up sample. *np* for each subgroup can also be found by multiplying the percent defective (*p*) by the total number of units in the subgroup (*n*). Note that *p* and *p*-bar are always used as ratios (not percentages) in the calculations. The value $\overline{p}$ is also called the process average. For a constant subgroup size *p* chart (where *n* is the same for all subgroups), $\Sigma n = mn$, where *m* is the number of subgroups. In the following example, $mn = 25(500) = 12{,}500$. Note that the Σn also equals 12,500.

$$\overline{p} = \Sigma np/\Sigma n = 167/12{,}500 \qquad = 0.01336 \ (1.1336\%)$$

$$\text{UCL}_p = \overline{p} + 3\sqrt{[\overline{p}(1 - \overline{p})/n]}$$

$$= 0.01336 + 3\sqrt{0.01336(1 - 0.01336)/500} = 0.029 \ (2.9\%)$$

$$\text{LCL}_p = \overline{p} - 3\sqrt{[\overline{p}(1 - \overline{p})/n]}$$

$$= 0.01336 - 3\sqrt{0.01336(1 - 0.01336)/500} = -0.0020\text{; use } 0.$$

3. Construct the chart and plot all 25 *p* values (see Figure 5.1). However, Figure 5.1 is only a partial chart. The real chart would be large enough for all 25, or more, subgroups (probably more because it should contain a whole month's worth of data). Remember to convert the central value (*p*-bar), the limits, and all plotted values to percentages (multiply by 100).
4. Display the chart in a conspicuous place and continue to measure and plot. Also continue to recalculate monthly. It is best for the operator to do the measuring and plotting, and to control the process.

L. A. DOTY CO.

Page ____ of _____

p CONTROL CHART

PART NO.: __________ PART NAME: __________

OPERATOR(S): __________

INSPECTOR(S): __________

PROCESS: __________ CHART NO: __________

GAGES: __________

SPECIFICATIONS: __________

DATE:	3/1	3/2	3/3	3/4	3/5	3/8	3/9

								TOTAL CHART TOTALS
# DEFECTS	17	5	13	6	5	0	11	183
1. Oversize	2	0	2	2	3	0	4	38
2. Undersize	10	4	8	3	0	0	6	111
3. Rough	5	1	3	1	2	0	1	34
4.								
5.								
# DEFECTIVES	15	4	11	4	3	0	9	167
# CHECKED	500	500	500	500	500	500	500	12,500
% DEFECTIVES	3.0	0.8	2.2	0.8	0.6	0.0	1.8	1.336

Figure 5.1. Sample constant *p* control chart.

VARIABLE SUBGROUP SIZE *p* CHARTS

This chart is identical to the constant subgroup size chart except that limits must be calculated for each subgroup. Actually this is also true of constant subgroup size charts. It's just that the limits are the same for each subgroup when the sample size is constant, making the resultant line a straight line, and making it unnecessary to calculate the limits for each subgroup (in other words, the control limits vary only according to the sample size, n). The formulas are identical for both charts — they are just used more often (for each subgroup instead of just once).

This chart should only be used when constant subgroup sizes are either impossible, unavailable, or unrealistic (which is very often true for nonmanufacturing, or service, type operations, or where operations are long and a day's production must be used).

Long process times present a special problem for attributes charts. It can be solved using one day's production as a lot size. This technique will be explained in conjunction with average p charts, below (although the technique is just as applicable to this chart). It's just that this technique is more apt to be used on an average chart rather than on a variable subgroup size chart.

Example 5.2.

Construct a variable p chart using the data in Figure 5.2.

Solution:

1. Collect the samples (subgroups), enter them onto the chart, and calculate the subgroup averages. This has already been done in Figure 5.2 for the first seven plots. The following calculation of the first subgroup average will be used as an example of these calculations.

   $p_1 = np/n = 26/450 = 0.058.$

2. Calculate the control limits for all 25 subgroups. This has already been done in Figure 5.2 for the first seven subgroups. However, the calculations for subgroup 1 shall be shown as an example. See step 2 of the solution to Example 5.1 for a definition of the symbols shown here.

   $\bar{p} = \Sigma np / \Sigma n = 309/11{,}208 \quad = 0.02757\ (2.757\%)$

   $UCL_{p1} = \bar{p} + 3\sqrt{[\bar{p}(1 - \bar{p})/n]}$

   $= 0.02757 + 3\sqrt{0.02757(1 - 0.02757)/450} \quad = 0.051\ (5.1\%)$

L. A. DOTY CO. Page ____ of _____

p CONTROL CHART

PART NO.: __________ PART NAME: __________

OPERATOR(S): __________

INSPECTOR(S): __________

PROCESS: __________ CHART NO: __________

GAGES: __________

SPECIFICATIONS: __________

	3/1	3/2	3/3	3/4	3/5	3/8	3/9	TOTALS
# DEFECTS	46	15	39	19	5	17	21	312
1. Fill	14	2	13	4	0	6	6	85
2. Burnt	25	9	20	11	3	9	12	179
3. Cold	7	4	6	4	2	2	3	48
# DEFECTIVES	26	7	25	8	2	11	5	309
# CHECKED	450	350	630	500	445	470	540	11,208
% DEFECTIVES	5.8	2.0	4.0	1.6	0.4	2.3	0.9	2.757
UCL	5.1	5.4	4.7	5.0	5.1	5.0	4.9	
LCL	0.4	0.1	0.8	0.6	0.4	0.5	0.7	

Figure 5.2. Sample variable *p* control chart.

$$LCL_{pl} = \bar{p} - 3\sqrt{[\bar{p}(1 - \bar{p})/n]}$$

$$= 0.02757 - 3\sqrt{0.02757(1 - 0.02757)/450} = 0.004\ (0.4\%).$$

3. Construct the chart and plot all 25 p values (see Figure 5.2). However, Figure 5.2 is only a partial chart. The real chart would be large enough for all 25, or more, subgroups (probably more because it should contain a whole month's worth of data). Remember to convert the central value (p-bar), the limits, and all plotted values to percentages (multiply by 100).
4. Display the chart in a conspicuous place and continue to measure and plot. Also continue to recalculate monthly. It is best for the operator to do the measuring and plotting, and to control the process.

AVERAGE SAMPLE SIZE *p* CHART (Also Called the Stabilized *p* Chart)

This chart is the same as the variable p chart, with variable subgroup sizes, except that an average subgroup size (n_a) is used to calculate the limit lines. Thus the limits can be represented as straight lines, restoring the predictive nature of the chart. Theoretically, the variation in subgroup sizes should be no greater than 25% in order to use the stabilized chart. However, in actual practice, the sizes can usually vary much more than this and still provide reasonable and effective control — just investigate all high values, whether inside or outside the limits. After all, the purpose of control charts is to reduce nonconformities. Since all entries on a p chart represent nonconformities, any investigation into causes, whether inside or outside the limits, should contribute to that goal.

This is probably the best chart for long production runs; where the sample size, at least when the chart is started, is one day's production. Long process times present an especially difficult problem for attributes charts. When process times are long, it just takes too long for an attributes chart to signal a possible out-of-control situation. Also, when process times are very long, each subgroup may take more than one day to complete. One way to avoid this problem is to use one day's production as the subgroup size (people usually have a difficult time remembering what happened more than one day at a time). However, there are two problems with this. First, a variable subgroup size, or average subgroup size, will have to be used (it would be very rare that a day's production would be the same size every day). In this case, a variable p or average p chart would be needed. Second, a day's production may not be large enough to constitute an acceptable subgroup size, so that too many of the samples would be likely to have zero defectives (and thus destroy the statistical viability of the chart).

At the start of such a chart, one day's production is used as a sample (or subgroup) size, and all production for that day is inspected (100% inspection). Thus, at the start of such a chart, the chart would not really be a statistical sampling chart. Instead it would record the results of a 100% inspection (although all statistical chart procedures would be used as if it were a regular statistical control chart). Later, as the process improves and the percent defective decreases, a sampling procedure using MIL-STD-105E can be instituted (one company has done quite well inspecting 25% or 13, whichever is higher, every time a lot reaches the inspector; even though the *p* charts are quickly reduced to mostly zeros). At this point, most of the samples would show zero defectives, and the chart would record mostly zero percent defective. This would not be a statistically viable chart, of course, but it can still be useful as a visible record of accomplishment. If at any time too many defectives are recorded, too many in accordance to MIL-STD-105E (see Chapter 8), 100% inspection would then be resumed until the process is brought back into control.

The formulas are still the same, except that one more formula is added to determine the average subgroup size. That formula is: $n_a = \Sigma n/m$, where n_a is the average subgroup size. This average subgroup size then replaces the n in the basic (constant) *p* chart formulas. The total number of subgroups is represented by m.

Example 5.3.

Construct an average *p* chart from the data of Figure 5.3.

Solution:

1. Collect the samples (subgroups), enter them onto the chart, and calculate the subgroup averages. This has already been done in Figure 5.3 for the first seven plots. The following calculation of the first subgroup average will be used as an example of these calculations.

   $p_1 = np/n = 26/450 = 0.058.$

2. Calculate the central value and the control limits. See Example 5.1 for a definition of the other symbols shown here.

   $p = \Sigma np/\Sigma n = 309/11{,}208 \quad = 0.0276\ (2.76\%)$

   $n_a = \Sigma n/m = 11{,}208/25 \quad = 448.3$

   $\text{UCL}_p = \overline{p} + 3\sqrt{[\overline{p}(1 - \overline{p})/n_a]}$

   $= 0.0276 + 3\sqrt{0.0276(1 - 0.0276)/448.3} \quad = 0.051\ (5.1\%)$

L. A. DOTY CO.

Page ____ of ____

p CONTROL CHART

PART NO.: ________ PART NAME: ________

OPERATOR(S): ________

INSPECTOR(S): ________

PROCESS: ________ CHART NO: ________

GAGES: ________

SPECIFICATIONS: ________

DATE:	3/1	3/2	3/3	3/4	3/5	3/8	3/9

								TOTALS
# DEFECTS	46	15	39	19	5	17	21	312
1. Fill	14	2	13	4	0	6	6	85
2. Burnt	25	9	20	11	3	9	12	179
3. Cold	7	4	6	4	2	2	3	48
4.								
5.								
# DEFECTIVES	26	7	25	8	2	11	5	309
# CHECKED	450	350	630	500	445	470	540	11,208
% DEFECTIVES	5.8	2.0	4.0	1.6	0.4	2.3	0.9	2.76

Figure 5.3. Sample average *p* control chart.

$$LCL_p = \bar{p} - 3\sqrt{[\bar{p}(1 - \bar{p})/n_a]}$$

$$= 0.0276 - 3\sqrt{0.0276(1 - 0.0276)/448.3} = 0.004.$$

3. Construct the chart and plot all 25 p values (see Figure 5.3). However, Figure 5.3 is only a partial chart. The real chart would be large enough for all 25, or more, subgroups (probably more because it should contain a whole month's worth of data). Remember to convert the central value (p-bar), the limits, and all plotted values to percentages (multiply by 100).
4. Display the chart in a conspicuous place and continue to measure and plot. Also continue to recalculate monthly. It is best for the operator to do the measuring and plotting, and to control the process.

THE CONSTANT SAMPLE SIZE *u* CHART (The Basic *u* Chart)

Defectives are controlled by the p chart and its adaptations. Defects are controlled by the u and the c charts and their adaptations. The u chart controls on the average number of defects per unit (u) for small sample sizes (average number of defects are charted), and is therefore called the "average" defects per unit chart. The c chart, on the other hand, controls on the actual number of defects for a single unit, and is therefore called just the defects per unit chart, since the c chart subgroup size is a single unit only ($n = 1$).

When the lower control limit (LCL) calculates to a negative number, it is changed to zero (there cannot be a negative number of defects). Also note that the number of defect types must equal the number of defects for that sample (for instance, 8 + 35 + 7 = 50). Defect types help to facilitate problem analysis; while the total number of defect types provide an almost automatic Pareto analysis.

Because we are using the Poisson approximation to the normal, the u-bar ($\bar{u}$) is equivalent to the mean (μ) of a normal distribution, while the square root of u-bar divided by n is equivalent to σ of the normal. The "3" in the formula refers to the number of standard deviations from the mean.

Example 5.4.

Construct a u chart from the data in Figure 5.4.

Solution:

1. Collect the samples (subgroups), calculate the u, the subgroup averages, and enter them onto the chart. This has already been done in Figure 5.4 for the first seven plots. The following calculation of the

L. A. DOTY CO. Page ____ of _____

u CONTROL CHART

PART NO.: __________ PART NAME: ______________________________

OPERATOR(S): ______________________________

INSPECTOR(S): ______________________________

PROCESS: ______________________________ CHART NO: ______________

GAGES: ______________________________

SPECIFICATIONS: ______________________________

DATE:	3/1	3/2	3/3	3/4	3/5	3/8	3/9

UCL = 1.35

$\bar{u}$ = 1.0432

LCL = 0.74

1.40
1.20
1.00
0.8
0.6
0.4
0.2
0

DEFECT TYPE	3/1	3/2	3/3	3/4	3/5	3/8	3/9	TOTAL CHART TOTALS
1. Oversize	8	15	6	34	11	2	21	387
2. Rough	35	40	63	70	46	14	50	1993
3. Undersize	7	13	4	24	22	7	38	784
4.								
5.								
# DEFECTS	150	68	73	128	79	23	109	2608
# CHECKED	100	100	100	100	100	100	100	2,500
DEFECTS/UNIT	0.50	0.68	0.73	1.28	0.79	0.23	1.09	1.0432

Figure 5.4. Sample constant *u* control chart.

first subgroup average (u) will be used as an example of these calculations. c is the total number of defects in the subgroup, n is the total number of units in the subgroup, and $\bar{u}$ (u-bar) is the average number of defects per subgroup in the start-up sample.

$u_1 = c/n = 50/100 = 0.50.$

2. Calculate the control limits and chart midpoint.

$$\bar{u} = c/n = 2608/2500 \qquad = 1.0432$$

$$\text{UCL}_u = \bar{u} + 3\sqrt{\bar{u}/n} =$$

$$1.0432 + 3\sqrt{1.0432/100} \qquad = 1.35$$

$$\text{LCL}_u = \bar{u} - 3\sqrt{\bar{u}/n} =$$

$$1.0432 - 3\sqrt{1.0432/100} \qquad = 0.74.$$

3. Construct the chart and plot all 25 u values (see Figure 5.4). However, Figure 5.4 is only a partial chart. The real chart would be large enough for all 25, or more, subgroups (probably more because it should contain a whole month's worth of data). Do not change to percentages (do not multiply by 100).
4. Display the chart in a conspicuous place and continue to measure and plot. Also continue to recalculate monthly. It is best for the operator to do the measuring and plotting, and to control the process.

THE BASIC *c* CHART

Defects are controlled by the u and the c charts. The u chart controls the average number of defects per unit (and so is called the "average" defects per unit chart), while the c chart controls the actual number of defects for a single unit (and is therefore called just the defects per unit chart). The subgroup size is a single unit only and, therefore, only the actual number of defects are charted.

Actually, the c chart is just a special case of the u chart for large units where it is more practical to use a single unit as the subgroup size. The formulas are identical to those of the u chart except that dividing by n is no longer necessary because n, the subgroup size, is now equal to 1 (also c is substituted for u in the c chart formulas). Since the subgroup size is 1, m (the number of subgroups) equals Σn.

When the lower control limit (LCL) calculates to a negative number, it is changed to zero (there cannot be a negative number of defects). Also note that the number of defect types must equal the number of defects for that unit (for instance, 2 + 8 + 1 = 11). Defect types help to facilitate problem analysis; while the total number of defect types provides an almost automatic Pareto analysis.

The c in the formula is equivalent to the mean (μ) of the normal distribution, while the $\sqrt{c}$ of the formula is equivalent to the standard deviation. The "3" refers to the number of standard deviations from the mean.

Example 5.5.

Construct a c chart from the data in Figure 5.5.

Solution:

1. Collect the samples (subgroups) and enter them onto the chart. This has already been done in Figure 5.5 for the first seven plots. Note that subgroup averages do not have to be calculated since the subgroup size is 1. Calculate the control limits.

   $$\bar{c} = \Sigma c/\Sigma n = \Sigma c/m = 127/25 \qquad = 5.08$$

   $$UCL_c = \bar{c} + 3\sqrt{c} = 5.08 + 3\sqrt{5.08} \qquad = 11.8$$

   $$LCL_c = \bar{c} - 3\sqrt{c} = 5.08 - 3\sqrt{5.08} \qquad = -1.68$$

   Use 0.0.

2. Construct the chart and plot all 25 c values (see Figure 5.5). However, Figure 5.5 is only a partial chart. The real chart would be large enough for all 25, or more, subgroups (probably more because it should contain a whole month's worth of data). Do not change to percentages (do not multiply by 100).
3. Display the chart in a conspicuous place and continue to measure and plot. Also continue to recalculate monthly. It is best for the operator to do the measuring and plotting, and to control the process.

OTHER ATTRIBUTES CONTROL CHARTS

(Although the following charts are not often employed in short run manufacturing, most of them are explained fairly thoroughly in Doty, 1996, Chapter 5.)

The *np* chart is the same as the *p* chart except that the actual number of defectives are plotted rather than the *p*'s. Therefore, the *p*'s do not even have to be calculated. The plotted values, then, are discrete, counted amounts and must, therefore, be whole numbers. Theoretically, this should also be true of the limits and the centerline. In actuality, though, the limits and centerline

L. A. DOTY CO.

Page ____ of ____

c CONTROL CHART

PART NO.: __________ PART NAME: __________

OPERATOR(S): __________

INSPECTOR(S): __________

PROCESS: __________ CHART NO: __________

GAGES: __________

SPECIFICATIONS: __________

DATE:	3/1	3/2	3/3	3/4	3/5	3/8	3/9

REVISED VALUES

UCL = 11.8

$\bar{c}$ = 5.08

LCL = 0

14, 12, 10, 8, 6, 4, 2, 0

DEFECT TYPE								TOTAL CHART TOTALS
1. Oversize	2	0	1	0	6	6	2	21
2. Rough	8	5	4	0	1	7	0	87
3. Undersize	1	0	0	0	1	0	0	19
4.								
5.								
# DEFECTS	11	5	5	0	8	13	2	127
# CHECKED	1	1	1	1	1	1	1	25
DEFECTS/UNIT								5.08

Figure 5.5. Sample *c* control chart.

are usually shown as fractions. (See the section entitled "Employee Rating" in Chapter 6 for an example of this chart.)

The variable *u* chart has a variable subgroup size instead of a constant subgroup size. Therefore, just as in the variable *p* chart, limit lines must be calculated for each subgroup (the limit lines, then, are not straight lines). Except for that, the formulas and calculations are the same (they just must be made for each subgroup instead of just once).

The average *u* chart, just like the average *p* chart, is the same as the variable *u* chart except that a new sample size — the average sample size, n_a — must be substituted for *n* in all of the formulas.

The weighted charts (weighted *p* and *u* and *c*) use a weighted measurement instead of the actual measurement (or observation). The formulas are somewhat complex and the charts are not used much, although they can be used with some success in nonmanufacturing and service applications.

The constant limit charts (for *p*, *u*, and *c*) have a constant upper and lower limit (3). The plotted points are just the number of standard deviations from the engineering mean for that product. Therefore, more than one product can be plotted on a single chart. These charts have several serious disadvantages: each of the plotted points is calculated using a very complicated formula, C_p values cannot be calculated, and the limit lines do not show process improvements.

— Chapter 6 —

CONTROL CHART ANALYSIS

There are many ways of analyzing problems. This chapter will explore the use and analysis of control charts for this purpose. Actually, there are 27 different control charts and over 100 different analyzing tools. The ones included in this book are the most popular and easiest to use.

A good analysis of a problem can almost always identify the problem and tell why it happened, and it can frequently give the analyst and others the solution direction — the type of solution needed — but it cannot tell what the final solution will be. That depends on the ingenuity and knowledge of the people involved, and on the solution costs. For a more complete analysis of this problem, see the section entitled "Observation" at the beginning of the next chapter.

The main purpose of a company — its reason for existence — is to produce a product or service that satisfies the customer. The purpose of SPC is to assist in the manufacturing of these products and services. It does this by assisting the production group in correcting the process, and in improving and changing the process parameters so that the process is better able to do what it has been designed to do. Such a process is considered to be in control, and a product from a process in control is also considered to be in control. Improving the process almost always means reducing the variation (the standard deviation). This is why variation reduction is so important to SPC.

A process can be a machine or group of machines; a delivery route; an investing procedure; a nursing procedure; an operating procedure; an accounting method; an irrigation and fertilization schedule; or whatever it takes to make the product or to provide the service.

USING CONTROL CHARTS

Control charts are used in several different ways (usually several at the same time). First, the chart is used to correct problems. The way this is done is to use information from the chart to identify problems and possible solutions. The types of problems identified for correction are those that cause the process to deviate from its intended use, that is, from its design. For instance, a product may have several units measure outside the control chart limits, or there may be patterns within the chart that cannot occur by chance alone (see the section on variable patterns, below). So corrective action is taken to restore the process to its original design, to see that the product measurement is not outside the control chart limits or that there are no identifiable patterns.

A process is "perfected" when it has zero variation over time — when all measurements are identical, day in and day out. Of course, this is impossible to actually achieve in real life, but it can usually be achieved in a practical sense, that is, close enough for all practical purposes. When this occurs, the process is considered to be "in-control," even though it may not be "perfected" (in other words, no assignable causes are present). "Perfection" (even though it can never be completely achieved) should always be the goal, and is the foundation of the SPC concept of continuous improvement — never stop trying to improve.

The next way that the chart is used is to provide information for changing the process by changing the process parameters. For instance, suppose that the process is a machine that is capable of producing the desired measurement to within ± 0.01 inches; this is called a "process parameter." Using information from the chart to keep the process within that design (±0.01 inches) is called "process correction." Using information from the chart to change that parameter (say from ±0.01 to ±0.005) is called "process change." The dimension can now be held closer to the process center, and to the specification center, than was before possible. The part is better, which may well lead to increased orders and increased profits (in fact, this is what usually happens in a case like this).

Please note that both of these practices ("process correction" and "process change") make improvements to the process, and therefore to the products made by that process. This is a great part of what SPC is all about — constant process improvement. Although both approaches tend to use the same tools, the problems tend to be different and the solution approach is different.

The next way a control chart can be used is to note when to change from a correction approach to a change approach. When no more corrections can be made, when the measurements are no longer outside the control limits, and there are no discernible patterns in the plots, the process is said to be stable (a highly desirable condition). Up to this time, any improvements were usually correction type activities, made mostly by the operator and foreman (of course, if a change is obvious, it could be made at any time). After this, the type of improvement activities must change from a corrections mode to a change mode (from just correcting the process to changing the process parameters). This is when top management must get involved (they may already have been involved to some extent, but the main responsibility for improvement rested on the operator and foreman). Top management must make some decisions as to what and how far, and must make some commitments as to resources (manpower, money, etc.). Control charts can show this important point to management.

Another way that control charts are used is to place them near the operator so that they provide a picture of the quality activities involved, assist the operator in finding new ways to produce the part better, and add precision and accuracy to the old methods. In this way, the operator and others get a visual picture of their quality improvement efforts. Even if the process is stable and no more improvements are possible, the chart posted at the process site can be a proud reminder to the operator, and others, of the quality successes achieved (it can also help keep the operator from reverting to the poor quality of yesterday). When performance (and quality) is measured, performance improves; when performance (and quality) is measured and reported, the rate of improvement accelerates.

Control charts can also be used to assist in identifying patterns for analysis. In essence, plot configurations are considered to be out of control if there is a greater than 1% probability that it can occur by chance alone. When this occurs, the configuration is called a pattern, and a search for assignable causes (also called special causes) should be instituted and, if found, corrected. It is important to understand that patterns refer to patterns of excessive variation. If all inspected units measured on the mean, there would be no variation, and no patterns. However, there are variations in everything — that's the way life is. Variations that are small and do not form any recognizable patterns are said to be caused by chance alone. But if the variation forms a recognizable pattern, and if that pattern can occur by chance alone less than 1% of the time (called, in quality, the 1% rule), the cause (or causes) is called an assignable (special) cause. These types of causes (assignable causes), then, should be investigated and eliminated. In general, chance variations, and causes, are considered to be acceptable, but assignable causes are not (variations caused by assignable causes are considered excessive and, therefore, must be eliminated). Patterns caused by excessive variations (assignable causes) are identified and listed in the following two sections.

ATTRIBUTES PATTERNS

Attributes chart plots are quite different from variables plots. Attributes plots always refer to nonconformities, that is, they are always outside the specification limits. Variables plots, on the other hand, consist almost completely of measurements that are inside the specifications limits (even when the plot falls outside the chart limits, it may not be outside the specification limits). The patterns, then, from these two charts are quite different.

There are only two types of attributes chart patterns that can be analyzed (unlike variables charts, which can have many types of patterns). The first is the out-of-control patterns — those plots that are above the upper limit. (Plots below the lower limit, if there are any, show superior quality, not inferior. They should be analyzed to see if the cause can be perpetuated.) Plots above the upper limit, of course, are assumed to have assignable causes which can be found and eliminated.

The second analyzable pattern is not actually found in the chart plots. This is the automatic Pareto analysis found in the section for kinds and amounts of defects. The totals column for these defects shows instantly which kind of defect occurs the most often. The analyst should then concentrate efforts toward eliminating these types of defects first. In this way, the analyst can usually realize the greatest rewards (cost improvement, usually) for the least expenditure.

VARIABLES PATTERNS

Variables charts, unlike attributes charts, can be analyzed for many different types of patterns. Also, unlike attributes charts, variables charts can show problems before defects occur. Thus the analysis of variables patterns can assist the analyst, and others, in eliminating causes (eliminating assignable causes) before they cause the products to become defective.

In essence, plot configurations are considered to be out of control if there is a greater than 1% probability that it can occur by chance alone (called the 1% rule in quality control). When this occurs, the configuration is called a pattern, and a search for assignable causes (also called special causes) should be instituted and, if found, corrected. These patterns (configurations of excessive variation) are as follows.

1. Any subgroup mean that falls outside of the control limits. Control limits are set at ±3 sigmas, so the probability that any in-control value will be outside of these limits by chance alone is 0.27% (1 - 0.9973). Since the distribution is symmetrical (control charts are derived from the normal curve), the probability that a value will fall above the upper control limit, from chance causes only, is one-half of 0.27% or 0.135% (the same is true for values below the lower control limit). The probability that more than one value will fall outside the control limits from chance alone quickly becomes astronomical — in other words, it is almost a certainty that something is wrong (the chance that 5 of 25 subgroups will be outside the limits, for instance, is 75 out of 10 billion!). Note that this pattern clearly satisfies the 1% rule (the probability is less than 1% that it could occur by chance alone). In fact, control limits can be set considerably below ±3 sigmas and still satisfy this rule (actually at ±2.327 or above). However, it has become customary for many years (since 1924) to use 6 sigma limits, probably due to the ease of calculation and the fact that it works.
2. Seven subgroup means in a row (see Figure 6.1). (This is also true of 10 out of 11 subgroup means in a row, or 12 of 14 in a row.) This can be 7 in a row above the mean, 7 in a row below the mean, 7 in a row alternating above and below the mean, 7 in a row going up, or 7 in a row going down (please note that Figure 6.1 shows only three of these five patterns). The mathematics of this pattern rule is as follows. Since, by chance alone, it is equally likely that any one value (subgroup mean) will be either part of the pattern or will not, the probability that any one value is part of a pattern is 0.50 or 50%. The probability that any two values are part of a pattern is then $0.5 \times 0.5 = 0.25$ (this is the product rule of probability that says that the probability of both is the product of their individual probabilities). If this logic is continued for 7 values in a row, the probability that all 7 are part of a pattern is $(0.5)^7 = 0.0078$ or 0.78%, obviously less than 1% (6 in a row is $(0.5)^6 = 0.0156$ or 1.56%, obviously greater than 1%). (Some say that the first point cannot be part of a pattern, and so the real pattern must be eight in a row instead of seven.)
3. Patterns between ±1 standard deviation from the mean, that is, either +1 σ above the mean or -1 σ below (see Figure 6.2). These patterns are: (1) 5 in a row, and (2) 6 of 7 in a row. Since control chart limits are set at ±3 standard deviations (6 sigmas; 6σ's), the chart can be divided into 6 equal parts, each one corresponding to the distance of a single standard deviation (except for some *R* charts that are truncated at zero). Standard deviations (σ's) follow the convention where

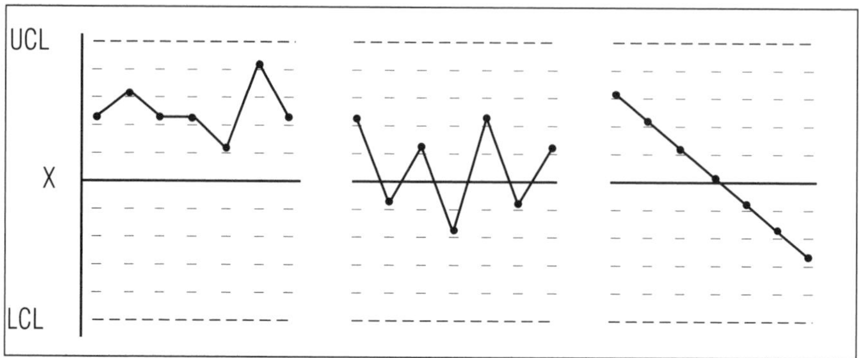

Figure 6.1. Control chart showing "seven in a row" out-of-control patterns.

those above the mean are considered to be positive (+) while those below are negative (-). The probability that any one value will fall within the first of these areas from the mean, either above or below the mean, is 0.3413 (0.50 - 0.1587; see Chapter 3 and -1σ from Table 1 at the back of the book). The probability that 5 in a row will occur is $(0.3413)^5 = 0.00463$, or 0.463%. This clearly meets the 1% rule's criteria for out-of-control (4 in a row = 0.0136, and therefore, fails the 1% rule). The mathematics for 6 of 7 in a row is somewhat complex and will not be given here. (Actually, this pattern is a very good one because the closer to the mean, the better the part. Therefore, any assignable causes identified here should probably be incorporated into the process in order to make the part better, to reduce the standard deviation.)

4. Patterns between +1 and +2 standard deviations from the mean or -1 and -2 (see Figure 6.3). These patterns are: (1) 3 in a row, and (2) 4 of 5 in a row. The probability that any one value will fall within either one of these areas is 0.136 (0.9773 at +2σ; - 0.8413 at +1σ, as can be seen in Table 1 at the back of the book). The probability that there will be 3 in a row, therefore, is $(0.136)^3 = 0.0025$, or 0.25% (which clearly satisfies the 1% rule). The mathematics for 4 of 5 is, once again, somewhat complex and will not be given here.
5. Two values in a row between +2 and +3 standard deviations from the mean or between -2 and -3 (see Figure 6.3). The probability that any one value will fall within either one of these areas is 0.02135 (0.99865 at +3σ; -0.9773 at +2σ). The probability that there will be 2 in a row, therefore, is $(0.02135)^2 = 0.0004558$, or 0.4588% (which clearly satisfies the 1% rule).
6. Groupings and long-term trends. Any pattern whose probability of being caused by chance alone is greater than 1%. This includes any long-term trend (up, down, alternating, etc.) that has an obvious pat-

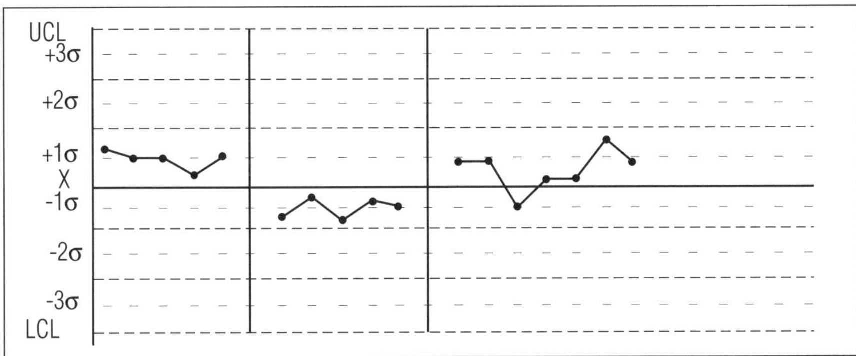

Figure 6.2. Control chart showing out-of-control patterns between ±1 standard deviations from the mean.

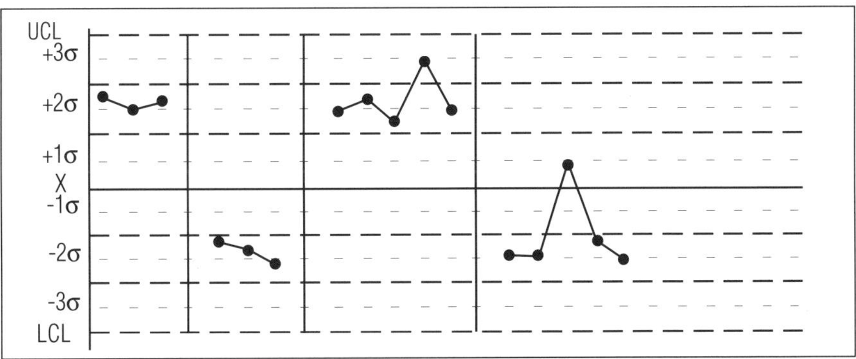

Figure 6.3. Control chart showing out-of-control patterns between 1 and 2 standard deviations from the mean.

tern, or if too many of the values group too close to the mean (more than 68.26% within + and - one standard deviation) with little or no values close to the limits, or too many values close to the limits, or too many values spread all over the chart (even if all are still inside the control limits).

CAUSES OF VARIATIONS

When analyzing control chart patterns, always be aware of the various categories of variation (it is variation, of course, that causes patterns, and out-of-control conditions). Each type of pattern often has essentially the same cause, especially in the same environment. Thus, once the cause of a particular type of pattern has been identified, it should be noted and then used for a guide in finding causes of similar patterns in the future. Eventually a check list of patterns and probable causes could be prepared that would greatly enhance pattern analysis activities.

The following causes and patterns occur mostly in a manufacturing setting, although with the proper change of names they can also be seen in nonmanufacturing and service processes.

1. *X*-bar versus *R*. When analyzing control charts, the general rule is to first correct the *R* chart (get it in control) before analyzing the *X*-bar chart.
2. Points outside the control limits (often called freaks). Look first for a possible measurement error and then for a sudden change in raw material.
3. Zone patterns (between the mean and 1σ, 1σ and 2σ, or 2σ and 3σ). Once again, look first for a measurement error and then for a sudden change in raw material. These patterns are also frequently caused by incomplete or missing operations.
4. Shifts (seven in a row above or below the center, or any long-term change in the process center). For shifts in the *X*-bar chart, look first for changes in materials or suppliers; and then for shift changes, changes in machine speed, or measurement error. In the *R* chart, look for operator problems or poor maintenance.
5. Cycles (seven in a row up and down, or any long-term up and down trend). Look for the same things happening over and over again, usually at the same time (time is often a dead giveaway for cycles). Look for such things as shift changes, new hires, defective equipment, fluctuating power, weather changes, and worker fatigue occurring at about the same time (fatigue is the most common cause of cycles in the *R* chart).
6. Trends (seven in a row up or down, or any long-term trend up or down or straight). Any up or down trend in the *X*-bar chart is bad, while a straight trend can be good, especially if it occurs at the center. However, an up trend in the *R* chart is bad, while a down trend is good. A straight trend in the *R* is mediocre. Good trends are usually caused by increased training and/or morale, better maintenance, increased experience, and better process controls. Bad trends are often caused by tired operators and poor maintenance. Bad trends in the *X*-bar chart can also be caused by tool wear.
7. Grouping and bunching. When this occurs in the *R* chart, it usually means that several distributions are represented (such as a mixture from two or more machines). When it occurs in the *X*-bar chart, almost anything can be happening. It is especially important when analyzing groupings and bunchings that the *R* chart be in control first.
8. Chart relationships. Sometimes a chart at one location on the production line is related to another at an earlier location. They could be measuring the same characteristic, or a different one that is related in

some way. This relationship can be positive (both charts go up and down together) or negative (one chart goes up when the other goes down). Analyzing both charts together can often give clues to the problem when a single chart analysis will not. Remember that the charts are often displaced in time so that a positive relationship may appear to be negative, and vice versa (because the earlier operation occurred before the latter). In this case, time must be factored into the analysis.

9. The process. This includes such things as poor workholding and positioning, machine vibration, machine looseness, hydraulic and electrical fluctuation, machine breakdown, machine wear, machine speeds and feeds, poor preventive maintenance, poor repairs, dirty machinery, wrong process used, poor setup, change in setup, poor fixture design, too much play in part positioning, incorrect use of fixture, etc.
10. The material. These types of variations are caused by differences in material characteristics, such as hardness, moisture content, tensile strength, ductility, hard/soft spots, too hard or too soft, high or low concentration, mixing of different lots, change in supplier and/or change in material, more than one supplier, etc.
11. The operator. This is perhaps the greatest source of variation. The personal, emotional, and mental problems of the operator, along with inattentiveness and lack of understanding, lead to misalignment, frequent machine adjustments, errors, improper handling, etc. Other operator problems are: new and/or untrained operator, operator fatigue (the most common cause of cycles in the *R* chart), change in shift, operator morale, etc. Probably 80% or more of quality problems are, or can be, solved by simply observing, or by asking the operator (getting the operator personally involved on a quality improvement team is by far the best procedure).
12. Tooling. Tooling problems can be caused by such things as: using the wrong tool, tool made incorrectly, tool used incorrectly, tool wear, etc.
13. Quality Control. If quality control inspectors do not fully understand the implications and proper uses of statistical control techniques, they can cause excessive variations by requiring too frequent adjustments to the process. This, along with faulty measuring equipment and incorrect measurements, can be a large source of variation in the product.
14. Measurement. These types of problems are caused by such things as: errors in measurement, using the wrong gauge, using an inaccurate gauge, misreading the measurement instrument, incorrect calculations, new and/or untrained inspector, etc.

15. Methods (procedures). Some common errors in this area are: incomplete operation, missing operation, wrong methods used, wrong methods specified, etc. A good production work order system can do a lot to reduce errors in this area.
16. Engineering. Engineering can cause variation through: incorrect or incomplete process designs, specifying engineering specifications outside the range of process capability, incorrect product specifications, unsafe product and/or methods design causing fear and hesitation on the part of the operator, and product design specifications unnecessarily critical (not "robustly" designed). (Robust means to design so that systems are not so dependent on changes in production, that is, so that changes in production do not cause very many errors.)
17. Management (systems or organizational errors). Most of the preceding causes of quality problems are systems or organizational errors and thus management causes. Most quality professionals estimate that as much as 95% of quality problems are systems or management controllable, not operator controllable (the estimate used to be 85% but it was revised in 1993).
18. Environment (temperature, moisture, sun, etc.).
19. Miscellaneous. Many very small variations in the product are caused by changes in temperature, humidity, light, air pressure, dust, etc. Sometimes, with certain products, these variations can be quite significant and require special procedures to control (for example, steam vents for humidity to control static in knitting mills, and the closing of certain windows during certain hours of the day so that the sun does not make the presses too hot).

CONTROL CHARTS AND SPECIFICATIONS

Control chart limits can be compared to specification limits to determine the process capability. It is important to do this so that Engineering can get information about how to design the product and about what the processes are capable of doing. It is also important to Production people who may need to change the process to make it easier, or even possible, to produce the product to specifications. Since specification limits only refer to measurable characteristics, this use is limited to control charts for variables.

There are two ways of making this comparison: by direct comparison, and by calculating process capability (C_P) ratios. The C_P ratios are explained in the next section. Direct comparison is done, basically, by entering the specification limits onto the control chart. Unfortunately, the specification limits must be changed in the same way that the control limits are changed in order to do this (due to the use of averages of small sample sizes rather than using individual values). C_P calculations do this automatically, as well as present a simple value for comparison. Because of this, the direct comparison method is seldom used. However, it will be presented for educational purposes.

There are three main types of direct comparisons, each requiring a different type of solution. The first case is when the control chart central value does not match the specification central value. This is the easiest of all process capability problems to solve since one of the central values can be changed to match the other one. Specifications, by their nature, cannot easily be changed (since they are determined by product and customer requirements). Therefore, it is the control chart central value that must usually be changed. In most cases, this is a simple matter of changing a machine setting. This might not be necessary, though, if the specification limits are far enough outside the control limits. However, even in this case, the centers should be matched, if possible. When centers are offset this way, there is always a potential for interference problems to develop.

If the specification limits are inside the control limits, or even close to them, instead of far outside, a lot of bad product is going to be produced. In this case, two problems must be solved simultaneously: first the central values must be matched, and then the process must be brought under control. In other words, the control chart standard deviation must be reduced so that the control chart limits are inside the specification limits.

The next situation is when the specification limits lie inside the control limits and the central values are equal (Figure 6.4). The farther the specifications limits lie inside the control limits, the higher the number of rejects that will be produced. For instance, suppose that the specifications lie at exactly ± 2 standard deviations from the mean. About 95% of the parts will be acceptable and 5% will not. At ± 1 standard deviations, only 68% of the parts will be usable. This situation presents a very difficult problem to

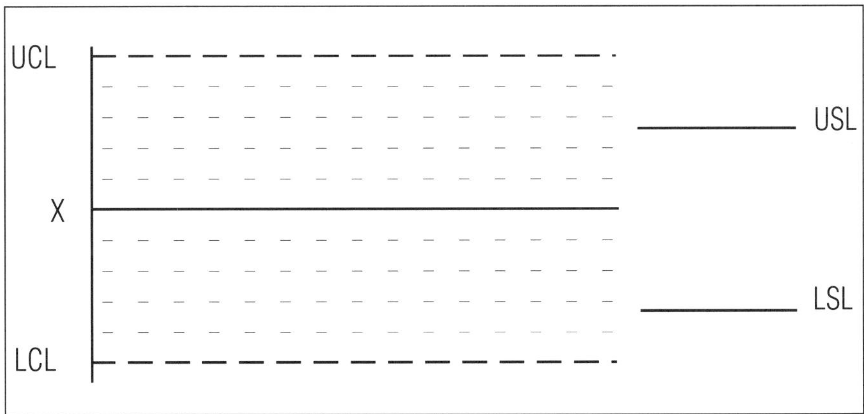

Figure 6.4. Control chart with specification limits inside the control limits.

management. Sometimes the specifications can be relaxed but this is rarely possible. Usually something has to be done to the process to reduce the variability (in other words, reduce the standard deviation; see the last two sections for a lot of causes and possible solutions). If these actions are not adequate, an entire new process and/or machine may have to be designed or purchased. It should be obvious that the solution to this condition can be quite expensive.

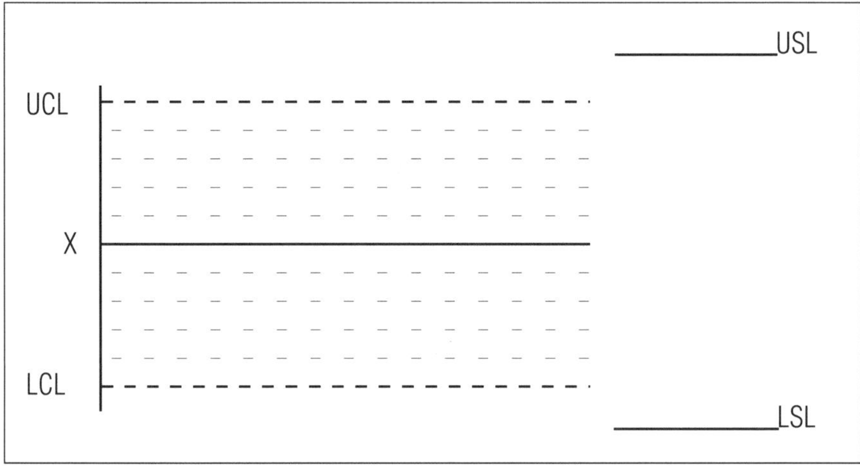

Figure 6.5. Control chart with specification limits outside the control limits.

The third condition exists when specification limits lie outside the control limits (Figure 6.5). This condition is usually not a problem, although it is always a good idea to keep the specifications far enough outside of the control limits to take care of any contingencies that might develop. Just how far outside depends on many factors, mostly product and production costs. A good rule of thumb is to have the specification limits extend about 1/3 the 6 sigma limits beyond the control limits (this is a C_p ratio of 1.33). This can be better controlled by calculating a capability ratio (as explained below in the next section).

PROCESS CAPABILITY (C_p) RATIOS

The comparing of specification and control chart limits is absolutely necessary, especially by Engineering. It gives information about how to design the product and about what the processes can do. It is also important to Production people who may need to change the process to make it easier, or even possible, to produce the product to specifications. Although the specification limits can be placed upon the charts as shown in the previous section, a better way is to calculate a process capability (C_p) ratio. This is just a mathematical relationship between the specification limits and centers and the control chart limits and centers. As was shown in the last section, it is best, by far, to have the control limits extend far beyond the specification limits (to minimize possible defects). It has been found that it is best to have the control limits about 1/3 larger than the specification limits, which is a C_P ratio of 1.33 (this corresponds to less than one part per million, that is, one bad part per million).

The C_{PK} value can give the analyst almost all the information needed, except the distance between the two centers. It takes a comparison between the C_{PL} and the C_{PU} to do this. If it weren't for needing to know how the centers compare, the C_{PK} would be the only process capability values needed. When the C_{PL} and the C_{PU} are equal, the two centers are identical. It is always best to make these two centers as close as possible, although it is almost impossible to be exact.

If any one of the capability ratios is below 1.00, or close to 1.00, the process is not capable of consistently producing good product (within the specifications). A capability ratio far above 1.00 (actually about 1.33 or above) is necessary (if this cannot be done, a normal curve economic analysis must be done to minimize scrap; see Doty, 1996, Chapter 6). The four capability ratios will be shown in relation to an example.

Suppose the USL = 1.168, LSL = 1.102, UCL = 1.152, LCL = 1.124, and $n = 4$. $\bar{\bar{X}}$ (X-double-bar), then, is 1.138 (½ of 1.152 + 1.124). The C_P ratios are:

1. $C_P = (USL - LSL)/[\sqrt{n\,(UCL - LCL)} =$

   $(1.168 - 1.102)/[\sqrt{4\,(1.152 - 1.124)} = 1.18.$

2. $C_{PL} = (\bar{\bar{X}} - LSL)/[½\sqrt{n\,(UCL - LCL)} =$

   $(1.138 - 1.102)/[½\sqrt{4\,(1.152 - 1.124)} = 1.29.$

3. $C_{PU} = (USL - \bar{\bar{X}})/[½\sqrt{n\,(UCL - LCL)} =$

   $(1.168 - 1.138)/[½\sqrt{4\,(1.152 - 1.124)} = 1.07.$

4. C_{PK} = lower of C_{PL} or C_{PU} = 1.07.

Note that this is short of the needed 1.33 C_P ratio. Also note that the C_{PL} and C_{PU} are quite different, which shows the difference in central values between the specifications and the control charts.

C_P = the basic capability ratio
C_{PL} = the lower one sided capability ratio
C_{PU} = the upper one sided capability ratio
C_{PK} = the lower of C_{PL} or C_{PU}
UCL = the upper control limit

LCL = the lower control limit
USL = the upper specification limit
LSL = the lower specification limit
$\overline{\overline{X}}$ = the process mean
m = the specification mean
n = the sample size.

PROCESS CAPABILITY ANALYSIS USING CODED DATA

When using coded data (such as in the zero-base models of Chapter 5), the C_P ratios must be calculated using coded data only.

Suppose that USL = 1.168, LSL = 1.102, UCL = 0.0162, LCL = -0.0098, and $n = 4$. $\overline{\overline{X}}$ (X-double-bar) is 0.0032 (½ of 0.0162 + -0.0098).

Before a C_P ratio can be calculated, the LSL and USL must be converted (coded). This is done by subtracting the specification central value from these limits. The center specification value does not have to be converted because it is always zero (0.00) when converted. The central specification value is 1.135 (½ of 1.168 + 1.102). The coded USL is 0.033 (1.168 - 1.135), and the coded LSL is -0.033 (1.102 - 1.135). Note that it is the coded USL and LSL that are used in the C_P formulas, not the real values.

The C_P values are:

$$C_P = (USL - LSL)/[\sqrt{n}\,(UCL - LCL)] =$$

$$[0.033 - (-0.033)]/[\sqrt{4}\,(0.0162 - \{-0.0098\})] = 1.27$$

$$C_{PL} = (\overline{\overline{X}} - LSL)/½\sqrt{n}\,(UCL - LCL)] =$$

$$[0.0032 - (-0.033)]/[½\sqrt{4}\,(0.0162 - \{-0.0098\})] = 1.39$$

$$C_{PU} = (USL - \overline{\overline{X}})/½\sqrt{n}\,(UCL - LCL)] =$$

$$[0.033 - (0.0032)]/[½\sqrt{4}\,(0.0162 - \{-0.0098\})] = 1.15$$

$$C_{PK} = \text{lower of } C_{PL} \text{ or } C_{PU} = 1.15.$$

Note that although the C_{PK} is above 1, it is below 1.33. This is short of the needed 1.33 C_{PK} ratio, although not by much. Also note that the C_{PL} and C_{PU} are different, showing the difference in the central values between the specification and the control chart.

PROCESS CAPABILITY ANALYSIS USING ATTRIBUTES DATA

The formulas shown above for process capability ratios obviously require measurable data. The only way to calculate a capability ratio for attributes data is to evaluate the data on a scale of some kind (1 to 10, 1 to 5, etc.). This type of measurement, however, almost always requires a great deal of independent judgment on the part of the person doing the measuring, and thus usually causes great measurement differences between analysts. Also, it is almost impossible to set specifications with this type of arbitrary measurement system. Therefore, capability ratios are, practically speaking, not possible for attributes data.

Actually, the only practical way to do any kind of capability analysis with attributes data is to determine a desirable central value (*p*-bar, *u*-bar, or *c*-bar) and compare this to the actual central value achieved by the process and shown on the chart. Upper limits cannot be compared this way because they can be arbitrarily changed by changing the subgroup size (as the subgroup size increases, the upper limit decreases, all else equal).

PARTS PER MILLION ANALYSIS

Process capability analysis can also assist in another modern production problem. Modern high technology requires such a high degree of quality and reliability that 6σ control limits are frequently inadequate today. A "parts per million" (ppm) of under 100 (and much less, in some cases) is now often being required. When compared to the ppm of 2700 for the basic control chart with 6σ limits (1-0.9973 = 0.0027 = 2700 parts per million), it is obvious that something better is needed. A high C_p ratio can help to offset this deficiency. In general, a capability ratio of 1.33 or greater comes pretty close to providing this protection (many are advocating 1.50 or greater).

A C_p ratio of 1.33 means that the tolerance limits (specifications) represent 7.98 sigmas ($1.33 \times 6\sigma$), or about ±4 standard deviations from the mean. The *Z* table (Table 1 in the back of the book) can be extended to this, although it only goes to 3.59 (extrapolation can also be used). A *Z* of 4.0, then, is approximately equal to a *P* of 0.9999, or a ppm of 100 (1 - 0.9999 = 0.0001 = 100 out of 1,000,000).

CONTROL CHARTS AND THE NORMAL CURVE

Control limits are determined in relation to sample size. They are meant to be used as control vehicles and cannot be used to determine actual areas under the curve. For instance, control limits (confidence limits in statistics) based on a sample size of 10,000 would have 1/50 the distance between them as would control limits based on a sample size of 4 (the difference between dividing by the square root of 4, or 2, and the square root of 10,000, or 100). However, they both have 6 sigma limits. We can be much more confident that our test answers are closer to the real universe value if our sample size is 10,000 instead of 4; and, therefore, we can use control limits that are very close to the test central value. Control limits derived from a sample size of 4, on the other hand, must be much further apart, due to the greater uncertainty involved.

A control limit, therefore, is a form of safety margin which changes as the incoming data change. The more data we have (the larger the sample size), the more certain we can be of our results, and the less safety margin we need (the limits can be closer). Figure 6.6 illustrates this relationship. The distribution of individual values (where the subgroup size, *n*, equals 1) is compared to distributions derived from subgroup sizes of 4 and 100. Note how the 6σ limits get closer to each other as the subgroup size is increased. Obviously, we cannot use control limits to determine what percent of items is likely to be outside the specification limit.

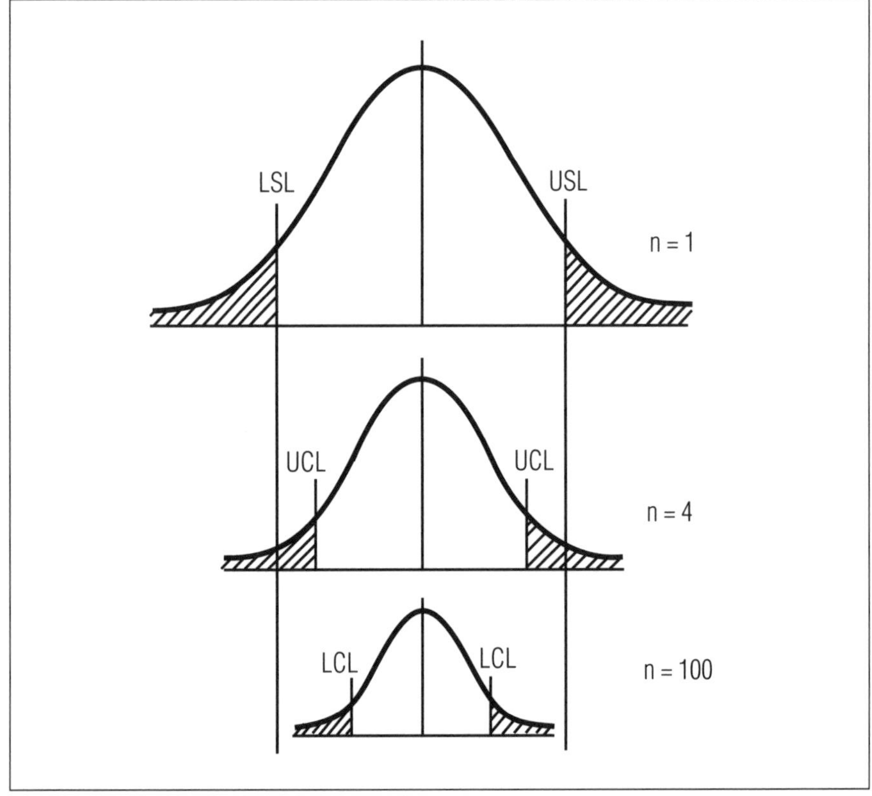

Figure 6.6. Comparison of control limits from different subgroup sizes.

EMPLOYEE EVALUATION

Control charts can be used quite effectively even for evaluating personnel (which is considered to be a nonmanufacturing duty — even if it occurs in a manufacturing area). Dr. W. Edwards Deming, in his book *Out of the Crisis* (see Deming, 1986, pp. 109 – 114), gives an excellent example of this. According to Dr. Deming, employee rating is constantly done incorrrectly by supervisors, mostly because they do not understand the implications and effects of statistical procedures. Dr. Deming's red bead experiment (duplicated below) shows clearly that merit increases can be extremely unjust (especially if neither statistics nor control charts are used). Dr. Deming says:

> "...apparent differences between people arise almost entirely from action of the system that they work in, not from the people themselves.
>
> If the work of a group forms a statistical system [none are outside the limits and there are no patterns], then the prize [special recognition for a job well done] would be merely a lottery . . . To call it an award of merit when the selection is merely a lottery, however, is to demoralize the whole force, prize winners included. Everybody will suppose that there are good reasons for the selection and will be trying to explain and reduce differences between [people]. This would be a futile exercise when the only differences are random deviations....
>
> What is worse, anybody that would seek a cause would come up with an answer, action on which could only make things worse henceforth."

Suppose that seven people draw 50 beads each, with replacement, from a box containing white and red beads (20% red). The aim is to draw white beads. Note that the *np* chart is used in order to make easy comparisons. The *p* could have been used but the limits would then have had to be compared to a *p* (9/60, 5/60, etc.) instead of the actual amount. (This problem duplicates Dr. Deming's red bead experiment.) The charted values are just the number of undesirable events (number of red beads). The results are:

Name	Red Beads (*np*)
1. Paul	9
2. Stephen	5
3. Karen	15
4. Brian	4
5. Debora	10
6. Keith	9
7. David	8
Total	60

Solution:

$\bar{p} = \Sigma n\,\bar{p}/\Sigma n = 60/(7 \times 50) = 0.17$

$n\,\bar{p} = 50(0.17) = 8.5$

$CLp = n\,\bar{p} \pm 3\sqrt{n\,\bar{p}\,(1 - \bar{p})} = 8.5 \pm 3\sqrt{8.5\,(1 - 0.17)} = 16.5\ \&\ 0.5.$

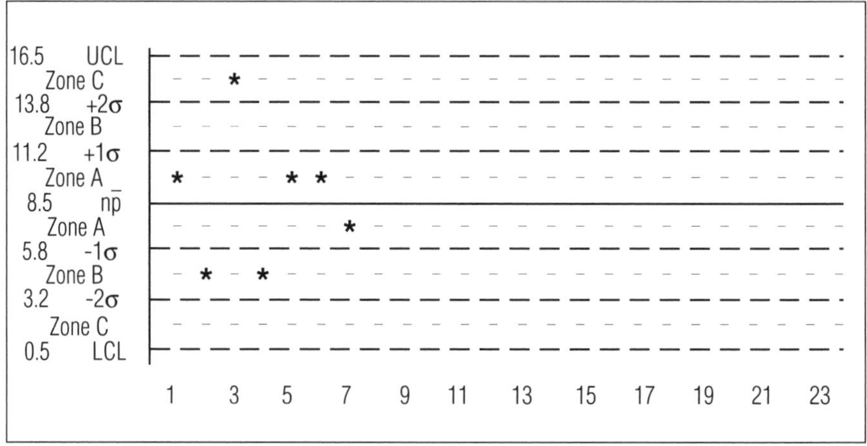

Figure 6.7. Employee rating control chart.

Since none of the people is above the upper limit of 16.5 nor below the lower limit of 0.5, the distribution is a chance one (occurring by chance alone), which it better be considering the nature of the experiment. (According to theory, there should be 25 entries, but in this case 7 is enough to show the trends, and to show just how bad ranking can really be.) Any deviation from chance causes in the above experiment would have had to result from some kind of cheating; such as removing the red beads and replacing them with white ones. Unfortunately, this is all too often the case with production — cheating is often used to offset the unfairness of management's evaluative procedures. Any reward or punishment based on ranking (a favorite management evaluation tool) would be unfair, and cause only resentment and, eventually, decreased performance (the opposite of the evaluation purpose). In ranking, Brian would have been rewarded (he only had 4 red beads) and Karen punished (she had 15 red beads). However, the number of red beads was obviously due to chance alone, not merit.

— Chapter 7 —

OTHER ANALYSIS TECHNIQUES

These are techniques (sometimes called tools) that do not need a control chart. Sometimes they can be used to find answers quickly, without a control chart, and sometimes they are used to find information that can be used with a control chart. They can be extremely helpful in finding quick solutions to problems. Because control charts can be somewhat complex, they can take some time to implement and to find the solution to a problem.

Actually, there are a great many techniques, or tools, that can be used by SPC. There are actually about 27 different types of control charts and over 50 techniques of other kinds (see Doty, 1996, Chapter 2), but the ones in this book are just the easiest to use, and the ones most often used for small lot manufacturing.

OBSERVATION

Control charts, of course, are the best way that SPC has of analyzing problems. But there are other ways. One excellent way is simply to observe. Problems can often be solved just by looking and using common sense (some have called it uncommon sense). For instance, there was the case of a machine producing too many defectives. An analyst went out and watched for a while and finally found the solution. The machine always produced the defectives when the sun began to shine directly on it through a window in the roof.

This example emphasizes the need for observation, and for using our wits. A simple observation can often negate the need for an expensive test or procedure. Also note that the analysis (even though it is a simple observation) directed everyone's attention to possible solutions. Although the solution seemed obvious, it was not, as the room needed the window for ventilation. The final answer, then, must depend on the ingenuity and knowledge of the people involved, and on the necessary costs. Just as obviously, top management must also get involved (if only to approve the costs, and maybe the solution method).

DEFECT LOCATION (MEASLES) CHART

This technique shows the location of defects on a graphic representation (a sketch or drawing) of the object. The position on the object can provide clues as to the cause(s). Figure 7.1 shows the two ways this tool can be used: a simple tally of defects (Chart A), and a categorization procedure (Chart B). This chart can also be combined with a Pareto and/or cause and effect analysis to determine degree of urgency (Pareto) and cause(s) of defects (cause and effect). Of course, it can always be used in combination with a control chart.

Chart A

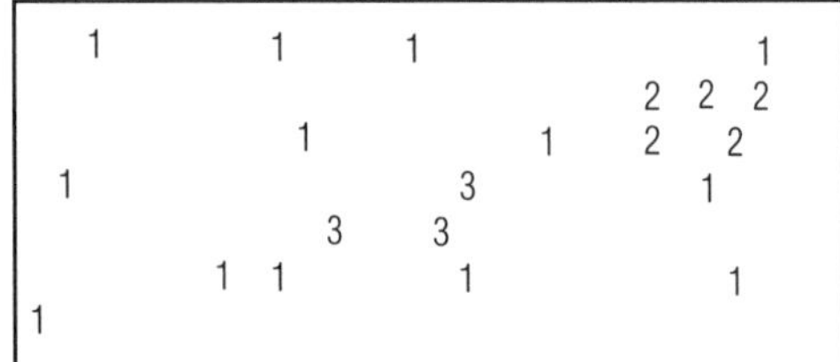

Chart B

Figure 7.1. Examples of a measles chart. The outline of the chart should be in the outline of the part.

PARETO ANALYSIS

The Pareto law is named after an Italian economist who observed that about 20% of the people had about 80% of the money. Because of this it is sometimes called the 80/20 rule. It illustrates the concept of the "vital few and the trivial many." The "vital few" refers to those things that affect us the most, that is, those that offer the greatest chance for the maximum return for our efforts. Since the vital few are larger in amount than the trivial many, it pays to concentrate on improving the larger base (it is easier to reduce a larger amount or to reduce it by a significant percentage). This rule, and its accompanying analysis, has an enormous number of applications in almost every aspect of life and work. For instance, in manufacturing it is usually true that about 20% of the products cause about 80% of the problems.

Many claim that two analyses should be made: a bar chart and a Pareto chart. However, a Pareto chart is just a bar chart arranged from high to low. It gives the same information but does it more quickly and obviously. As such, it gives us an instantaneous picture of the relationships involved; a picture that instantly identifies those problems we should address first (one look tells everyone what and/or where the major problem is). Therefore, a Pareto chart should almost always be used in place of a bar chart. (However, when a bar chart is used as a histogram, it can show various shapes that will give information about problem causes and possible solutions; see the later section of this chapter called "Histograms.")

Since the objective of Pareto charts is improvement of the process, many Pareto analysts will use two charts showing the before and after conditions, before and after improvement (Figure 7.3). As with almost all quality tools, the construction and use of Pareto charts can be greatly enhanced by the use of teams and an independent facilitator.

Pareto charts are constructed so that the count, or measurement, is on the left-hand side of the vertical axis, and the categories being counted are on the horizontal axis. Many charts also have the percent of total count on the right-hand side of the vertical axis. Some of the quality-type categories are: operators, work groups, type of products, sizes, type of damage, type of defect or defective, type of injuries, cost, contribution to profit, etc. The count, or measurement, of the category can also be coded for severity, but this is rather difficult and not of significant benefit to short run manufacturers.

An example will be used to show how Pareto charts can be used. In the example (Figure 7.2), the tally (count) is the number of errors made by each person. The percent (%) is calculated by dividing each count by the total (50) and then multiplying by 100 (for instance, the first percentage is 22/50 = 0.44 or 44%). The cumulative percent (CUM %) is calculated by adding down the line (for instance, 64 = 44 + 20; 80 = 64 + 16, etc.). The bars show the counts and percentages (%) and the line shows the cumulative percentages (CUM %). Actually, the analysis can be made without the line, and without the cumulative percent (CUM %). However, most Pareto charts are shown this way. The operator number below shows how the people being evaluated have been arranged from high to low.

Operator	Tally	Count	%	CUM%
4. Brian	1111111111111111111111	22	44	44
2. Stephen	1111111111	10	20	64
6. Keith	11111111	8	16	80
1. Paul	1111	4	8	88
7. David	1111	4	8	96
5. Debora	11	2	4	100
3. Karen	0	0	0	100
Totals		50	100	

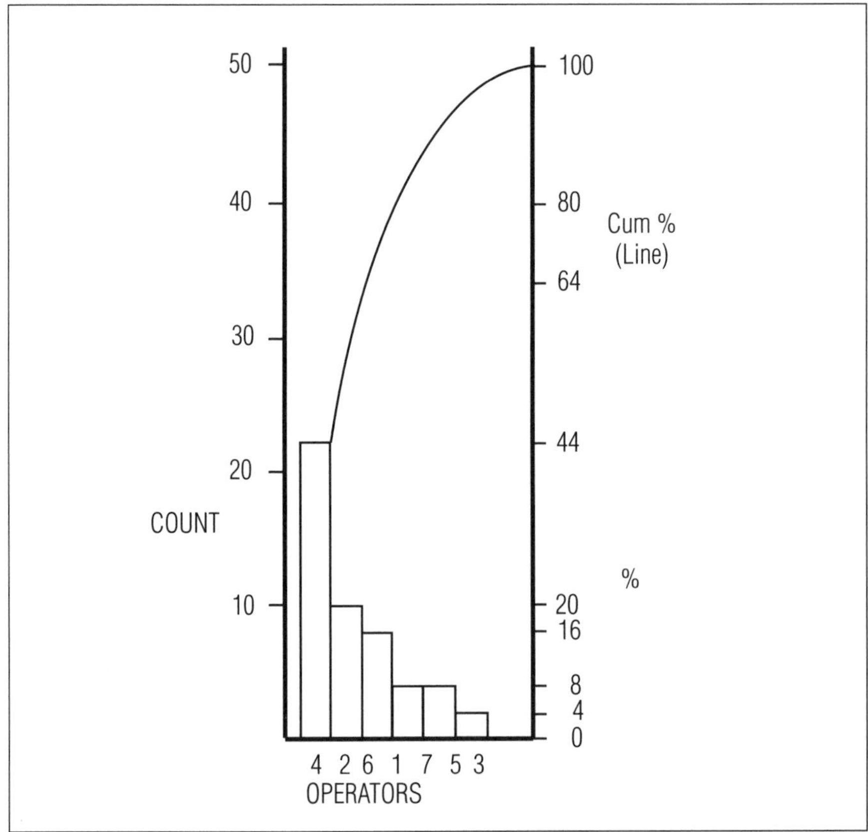

Figure 7.2. Basic Pareto chart using counts, percent, and cumulative percent.

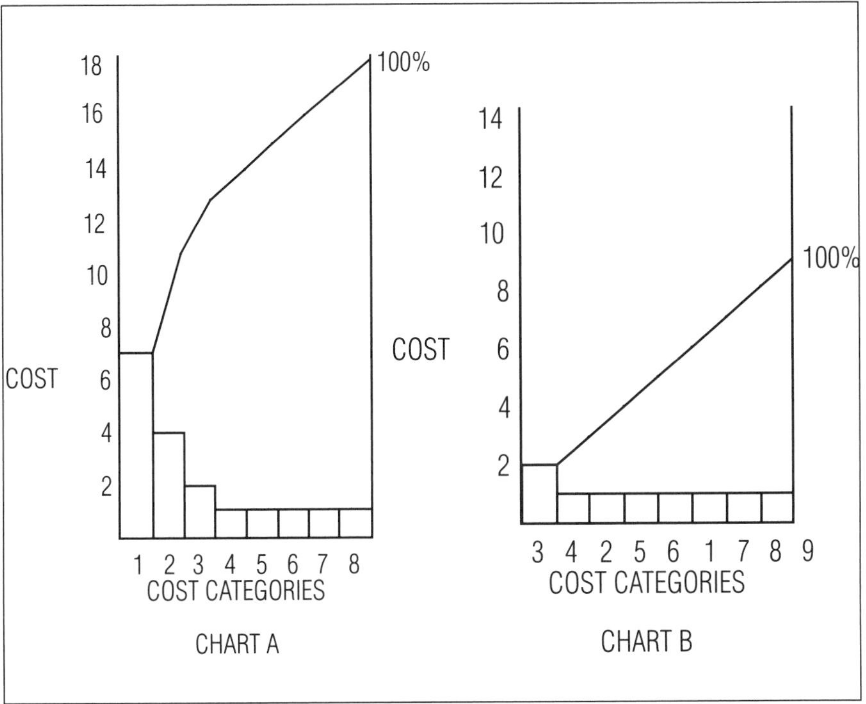

Figure 7.3. Pareto charts showing cost reductions from Chart A to Chart B.

Pareto charts are often used to illustrate change, as can be seen in the Cost Reduction Charts in Figure 7.3. In this instance, causes for high costs were identified, the process was improved, and the resultant reduction is graphically demonstrated by comparing the two charts.

In another example of Parato analysis (Figure 7.4), the actual problems have been "coded" (to letters A, B, etc.) to protect the source. Prior to the analysis, it was widely believed that the problem was part F, and possibly E as well, due to the type of information and the way it was being received. The Pareto analysis showed that the real problem was A and B. Problems in A and B are highly interrelated, and solving one tends to solve the other. Also, solutions to the A and B problems tend to solve E and F problems as well. However, the opposite is not true; apparent solutions to E and F problems seldom help in solving A and/or B problems. Also note that A and B were considerably higher than E or F. Obviously, something was wrong there. Once the real nature of the problem was uncovered, the incidence of defective units in this area dropped from 7% to less than 0.5%. This is an example of how properly diagnosed information can change the nature of "preconceived" ideas (change the bias). Much time and effort was lost in trying to solve the problem from the wrong direction.

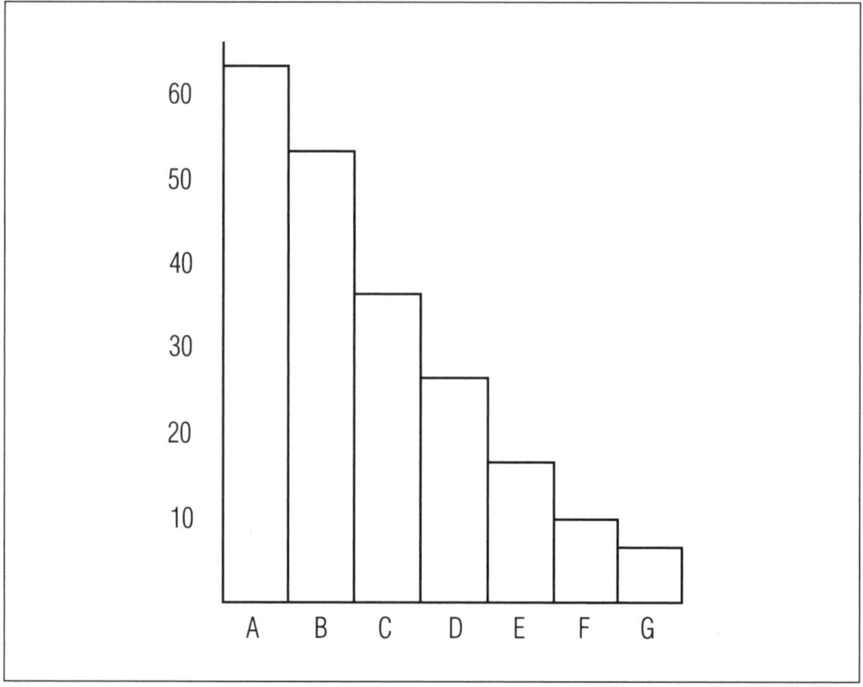

Figure 7.4. Pareto chart using coded analysis.

CAUSE AND EFFECT DIAGRAM (FISHBONE CHART OR ISHIKAWA DIAGRAM)

As the name implies, this tool is a group of causes and effects diagrammed to show the interrelationships. The diagram is a form of tree diagram on its side so that it looks like a fishbone (see Figure 7.5). The distinctive diagram is named for its inventor, Kaoru Ishikawa.

To form an Ishikawa diagram, begin by stating the problem in the form of an effect. In Figure 7.5 the problem is to maximize the surface finish of a product, within limits. Smoothness, then, is the main effect. Lines are then extended up and down at an angle from the center line, and main causes are identified and placed at the end of the lines. These main causes are usually some form of direct manufacturing factors including materials, equipment, work methods, operators/workers, processes, tooling, management (policies), measurement, and environment. The first three usually account for 80% of all problems.

Each of these primary causes is now treated as effects, and secondary causes are identified for each of them, then each of the secondary causes is treated as effects and causes found for each of them, and so on. The procedure is repeated until all causes are identified.

Each cause, no matter where placed on the chart, must relate to the main effect (such as the effect "smoothness" in Figure 7.5). If the chart becomes overly complex and extensive, secondary charts can be constructed from any of the causes. That cause then becomes the primary effect of the secondary chart (on the main chart always note where a secondary chart appends, and on the secondary chart where it appends on the main chart).

The preferred method for determining causes and effects is to form a team of those most directly concerned with the main problem and then use the brainstorming procedure. Any quality characteristic (such as length, hardness, percent defectives, people, etc.) can become an effect around which a cause and effect chart can be constructed. However, in the event that the problem is people (how to modify behavior, for instance), consider identifying a desired result (a goal) rather than a problem, as the main effect. In other words, concentrate on the characteristics that must be achieved rather than on how to change people, because criticism can degenerate into confrontation, resistance, decreased morale, etc., rather than improvements in quality.

Cause and effect diagrams are especially effective in facilitating the brainstorming procedure because they encourage examining and analyzing the processes (the root of all quality improvement lies in understanding the process) and planning procedures, and they contribute to determining the causes of dispersion. They are also used quite extensively by design engineering.

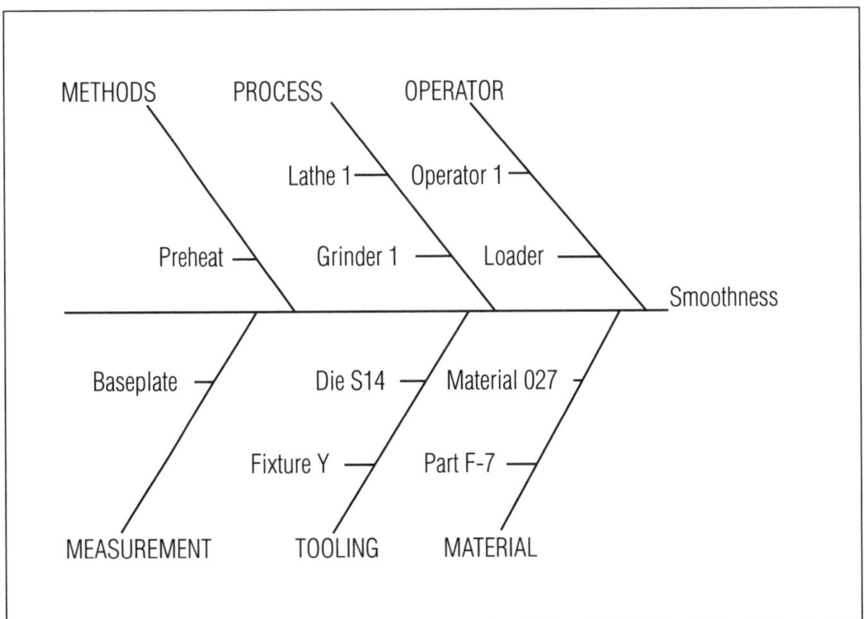

Figure 7.5. Basic cause and effect diagram.

HISTOGRAMS

A histogram is a special kind of bar chart. A simple bar chart (as described in the section above entitled "Pareto Analysis") is just a group of bars arranged on a chart as to counts. In a histogram, on the other hand, the measurements are first divided into groups, then arranged from low to high, and then their averages placed onto a chart. This is the same method that control charts use.

Actually, many people call all bar charts histograms, even those that simply record the error counts (as in Pareto charts, above), but it is better if they are thought of as separate charts. A Pareto chart is always a simple bar chart, arranged from high to low. A histogram, on the other hand, is much more complicated, and takes some special techniques to construct. A method for constructing histograms, using averages of small samples, is given in the next section of this chapter.

Histograms, especially their shapes, can be used to convey information for analysis, and to provide information for the reduction of variation. These shapes are as follows.

1. Bell-shaped (normal, Gaussian). This is the normal, natural, pattern of data from control charts. Any deviations from this pattern are usually abnormal in some way (and can be assumed to have assignable or special causes) and can usually, therefore, provide clues about the variation. Even when the pattern is normal, however, it may still be possible to reduce the variation by decreasing the width of the distribution — by decreasing the standard deviation (see Chapters 3 and 6).
2. Bi-modal (two peaks — the peaks do not have to be the same height). This distribution is most commonly a mixture of two processes (a combination of two distributions) such as identical parts from two different machines as shown in Figure 7.6.
3. The plateau distribution (fairly flat on top, with very slight tails). This usually results from a mixture of many different processes. It can be analyzed by diagramming the flow and observing the processes. See Figure 7.7.
4. The comb distribution (alternating high and low values) is illustrated in Figure 7.8. This distribution can be caused by errors in measurement, errors in the organization of the data, and/or rounding errors.
5. The skewed distribution (a long tail on one side, normal on the other). When the long tail is to the left, the distribution is negatively skewed; if to the right, it is positively skewed. Neither is necessarily bad. Many skewed distributions occur naturally with certain types of data and can be regularized with their own formulas (Poisson, log-

normal, exponential, etc.). However, if the long tail is seen to have a negative impact on quality, the process should be investigated so that the cause can be determined and eliminated. Some of the causes of skewed distributions are: short cycle tasks, one-sided specification limits, and practical limits on one side only. See Figures 7.9 and 7.10.

6. The truncated distribution (a smooth curve that ends abruptly on one side). External forces to the process, such as screening, 100% inspection, or a review process, are often the cause. Truncating usually indicates added costs and is therefore a good candidate for improvement. The truncated distribution is shown in Figure 7.11.
7. The isolated peak distribution (a small, separate, but obvious group of data to one side of the parent group). Caused by poor inspection, measurement errors, or data entry errors. See Figure 7.12.
8. Edge-peaked distribution (a peak right at either edge). This usually happens when data from an otherwise long tail have been lumped together at one point (data from outside the limit have been recorded as being inside the limit). See Figure 7.13.

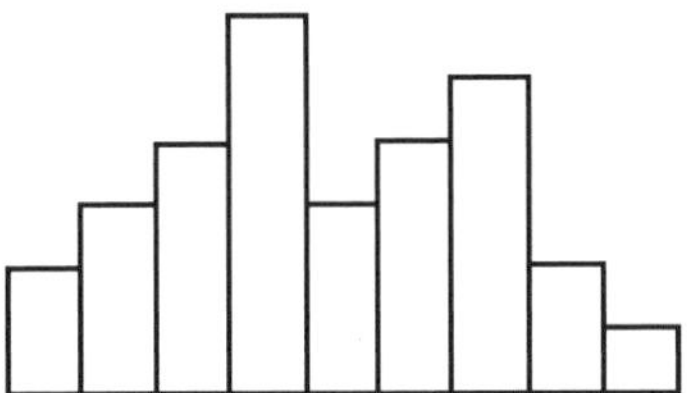

Figure 7.6. Bi-modal distribution.

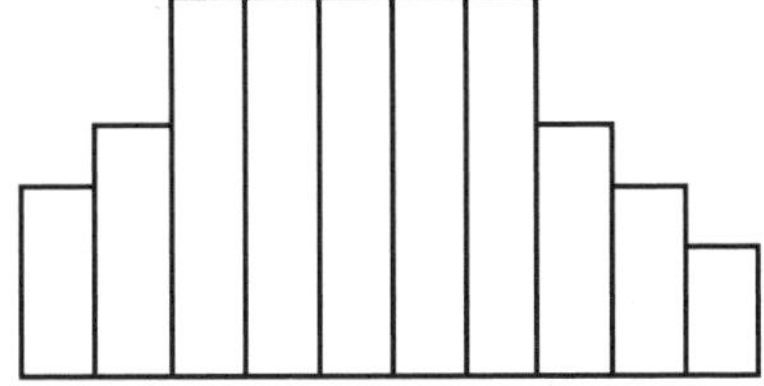

Figure 7.7. Plateau distribution.

Figure 7.8. Comb distribution.

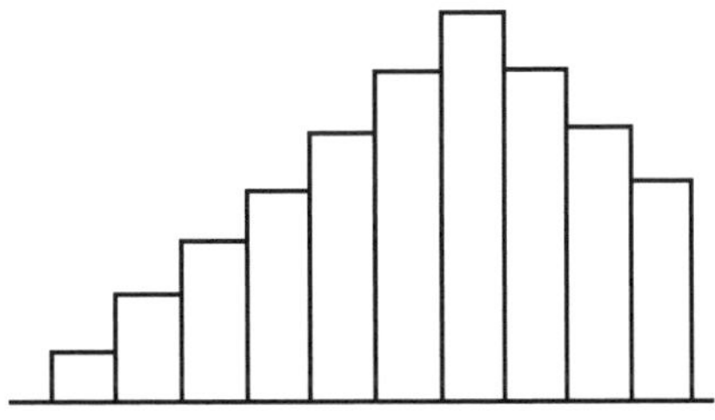

Figure 7.9. Skewed to left.

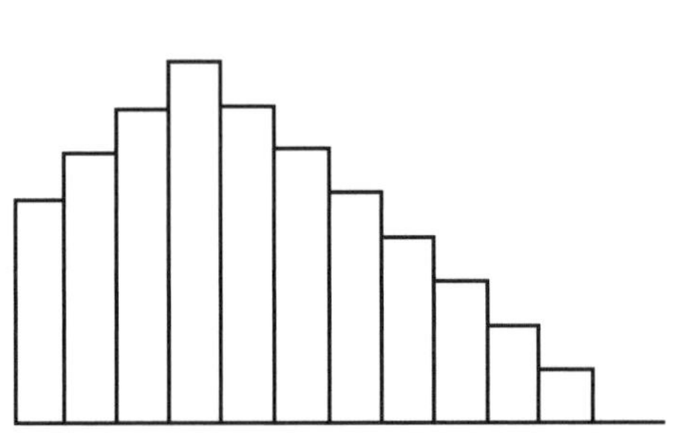

Figure 7.10. Skewed to right.

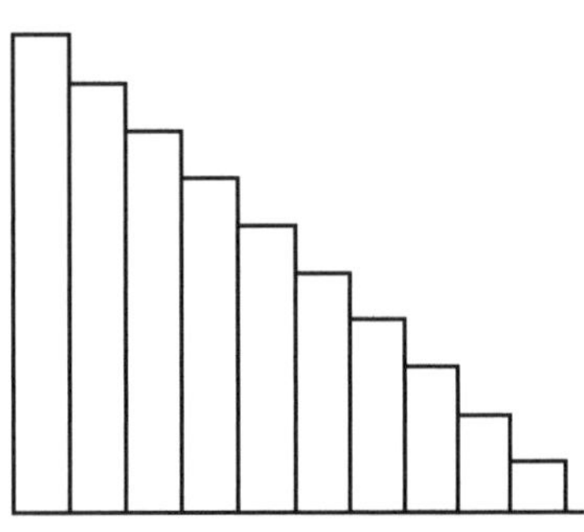

Figure 7.11. Truncated distribution.

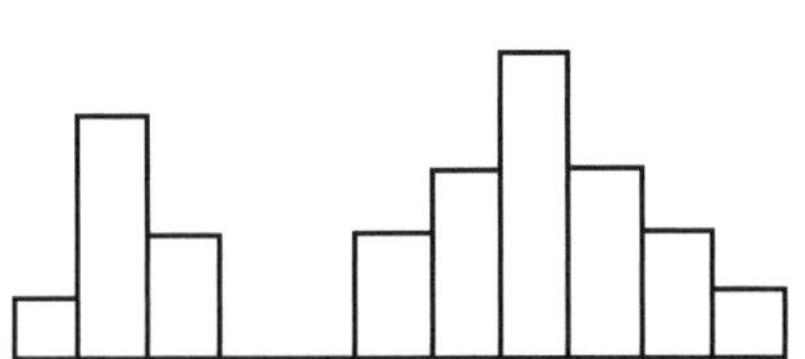

Figure 7.12. Isolated peak distribution.

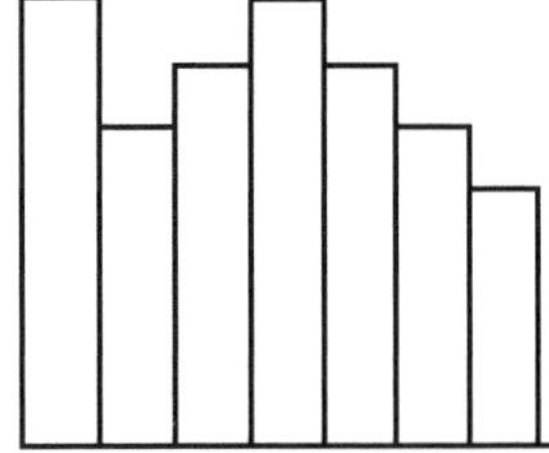

Figure 7.13. Edge-peaked distribution.

CONSTRUCTING HISTOGRAMS

To facilitate the handling and pattern analyses of large amounts of data (as in the section above on Histograms, and in Chapter 3), the data must usually be arranged in some manner. There are many alternatives that may be used, but one of the best ways is to organize the data into frequency groupings (also known as cells). Table 7.2 shows an example of such a grouping derived from the raw data of Table 7.1.

Table 7.1 Shaft Diameters (inches)

Sample	Measurements (observations)			
1	2.48	2.49	2.54	2.48
2	2.61	2.71	2.64	2.67
3	2.57	2.67	2.59	2.65
4	2.49	2.68	2.57	2.68
5	2.54	2.65	2.56	2.57
..	....	....	....	....
..	....	....	....	....
25	2.65	2.64	2.65	2.49

Table 7.2 Frequency Distribution of Shaft Diameters

Cell Boundaries	Midpoints	Frequency	Tally
2.47 — 2.51	2.49	3	111
2.52 — 2.56	2.54	16	1111111111111111
2.57 — 2.61	2.59	35	11111111111111111111111111111111111
2.62 — 2.66	2.64	27	111111111111111111111111111
2.67 — 2.71	2.69	9	111111111
2.72 — 2.76	2.74	5	11111
2.73 — 2.81	2.79	3	111
2.74 — 2.86	2.84	1	1
2.87 — 2.92	2.89	1	1

The following steps are used to organize data into a frequency grouping.

1. Collect the raw data. This has been done and is displayed in Table 7.1. Note that this table is not complete, but it contains enough information to demonstrate how the data are organized into the cells of Table 7.2. In Table 7.1, the data have been collected in a particular order, which is in a characteristic pattern easily recognizable by any Quality Control or SPC practitioner. Each line contains four measurements of a particular characteristic on four parts that were consecutively manufactured. However, it makes no difference how the data are collected or displayed in order to convert them into cells (as in Table 7.2).
2. Determine the range of the data.

   $R = X_H - X_L$ = High - Low = 2.91 - 2.48 = 0.43.
3. Choose the cell interval and determine the number of cells (they are interrelated and must be determined together by trial and error). The cell interval is the uniform interval between cells; it is the difference between successive lower boundaries, successive upper boundaries, or successive midpoints. In Table 7.2, for instance, the interval is 0.05 inches (2.52-2.47; 2.56-2.51; 2.54-2.49; 2.57-2.52; etc.). The cell interval must conform to two rules: it must be an odd number, and it must have the same number of decimal points as the original data. This allows for the cells to be organized in such a way that the midpoints also have the same number of decimal points as the original data. The procedure is as follows.
   a) Divide the range (R) by successively larger odd numbers, starting with the digit 3 at the rightmost digit (that is: use 3, 30, etc., for a range that has no decimals; 0.3 for a range with one deci-

mal; 0.03 for 2 decimals, etc.; depending on the number of decimal points in the original data). Each divisor represents a possible cell interval, and the result of each division represents a possible number of cells.

b) Continue these divisions until a result exactly matches the square root of the sample size (not the subgroup size), or is finally smaller than this square root (the result — number of cells — will decrease as the divisor, or cell interval, is increased). The sample size in Table 7.1, for instance, is 100, so the square root is 10.

c) If the number of cells calculated is not a whole number, round up to the next whole number (never round down), since there cannot be a half a cell (or 1.5, or 2.5, etc.). If the number of cells is rounded down, the highest cell will not have enough room for all the data. If rounded up, some of the data points at the end of the highest cell will be empty — no measurements will be available for those particular numbers. In order to maintain normality (keep the curve normal), these empty data points must be evenly divided between the lowest and highest cells. The procedure for allocating these empty data points will be explained later.

d) Choose that cell interval which has the number of cells closest to the square root of the sample size. If two are equally close, choose the one that has the lowest number of cells.

e) The cell interval will be that number used in the divisor for determining the number of cells actually chosen for the grouping. The calculations for Table 7.1 are:

   0.43/0.03 = 14.3 or 15 cells
   0.43/0.05 = 8.6 or 9 cells.

Since 9 is less than the square root of the sample size of 100, the successive divisions can stop here. And since 9 is closer to 10 (the square root of 100) than is 15, choose 9 as the number of cells and 0.05 as the cell interval (note that if 15 had been chosen as the number of cells, the cell interval would have been 0.03).

4. Choose the lower boundary of the lowest cell. This is the procedure for allocating empty data points between the lowest and highest cells (if rounding had been necessary). The amount of allocation depends on the amount of rounding done. Just divide the empty data points between the high and the low. The following formula does this, and also gives the lower boundary that must be used (remember to always round up). In the formula, i = cell interval and C = the number of cells.

X_L - [($C \times i$) - R]/2 = lower boundary.

If the resultant answer is equal to or greater than the lowest measurement (X_L), then use the lowest measurement. For our problem, the necessary lower boundary of the lowest cell is:

2.48 - [(9 × 0.05) - 0.43]/2 = 2.47.

5. Determine the upper boundary of the lowest cell. This is done by adding the cell interval to the lower boundary and subtracting 1 from the last digit. This subtraction differentiates between the upper boundary of the previous cell and the lower boundary of the next cell (however, this digit must be added back later to the upper boundary of the highest cell). The upper boundary of the lowest cell for Table 7.1 is:

   2.47 + 0.05 - 0.01 = 2.51.

6. Determine the midpoint of the lowest cell. This is the assumed average of the cell (all measurements within the cell are assumed to have this value). In Table 7.2, for instance, three values are assumed to equal 2.49 each, 16 values are assumed to equal 2.54 each, etc. The real average may be, and usually is, lower or higher than the midpoint; but if the sample size is large enough (100 or more), errors in one cell will usually be offset enough by opposite errors in other cells so that the final result is close enough for all practical purposes (the statistical concept of compensating variations). The midpoint is calculated by adding the upper and lower boundaries and dividing by two. The midpoint of the lowest cell of Table 7.1, then, is:

   (2.47 + 2.51)/2 = 2.49.

7. Determine the remaining boundaries and midpoints. This is accomplished by adding the cell intervals successively until the highest data value is included in the final cell. In Table 7.1, the boundaries and midpoint of cell 2 are:

   2.47 + 0.05 = 2.52 (lower boundary)
   2.51 + 0.05 = 2.56 (upper boundary)
   2.49 + 0.05 = 2.54 (midpoint).

   These calculations then continue until the ninth cell is complete. The upper boundary of the last cell, however, must be adjusted to offset the one digit subtraction started at the first cell. Just add 1 to the last digit. For our example, the upper boundary of the ninth cell is: 2.86 + 0.05 + 0.01 = 2.92 (although this last calculation is not mathematically correct, it works, and is much easier than the more mathematically correct method).

8. Tally the data; determine the frequency of each cell (it may be helpful to first arrange the data in ascending or descending order).
9. List the cell boundaries in order from low to high, along with their associated midpoints and frequencies, as in Table 7.2, and tally. Putting lines around the tally gives a histogram (although on its side — a histogram is usually up and down rather than sideways). Since the lines, in this case, were made by a computer, the tallies and histogram are to scale.

It is also possible to group by individual values rather than cells. This would occur if the number of individual values is small in amount, say less than 20. In this case, each individual value (measurement or count) becomes the equivalent of a cell midpoint and there are no cell boundaries. The steps to organizing this type of data are quite simple; just tally the data for each possible value (some of the data points may have zeros). In this case, the number of cells become one more than the range ($R + 1$).

BRAINSTORMING

Brainstorming is a free, unfettered blitz of ideas, thoughts, and suggestions, especially about problems and possible solutions to problems (including solving quality problems). Brainstorming must be done with teams of four to eight (preferably five). With SPC, this can just be a discussion of a few of those directly responsible, or it can be more formal — with those directly responsible retiring to a room where each can have a turn stating his or her ideas and/or possible solutions. A scribe will write down the ideas and any notes, and then display these prominently so that all can see them. Then each member should comment on each idea, combining ideas if necessary (combined ideas would, of course, be a new idea to consider). Finally, the team should vote on the best ideas (probably make a list from best to worst, in the order of acceptability). All voting should be private; no one must know how any one member voted. An even more formal procedure would use a permanent team and a facilitator.

Some important principles are as follows.

1. No judgment or criticism — not even such things as "isn't that the same thing as Joe just said?"
2. The more ideas produced, the greater the chance of useful comments.
3. Many minds are better than one; many ideas are better than one. Quantity, in this respect, is more important than quality.
4. The free flow of ideas must be uninhibited. Each idea may start another, even if it seems ridiculous. Also, ideas may be combined into new ideas.

5. Brainstorming can be used at any of the problem-solving steps, or stages.
6. It is best, in brainstorming, to just make a bare statement of the problem. Take no chances on generating bias in the team members.
7. As the members take their turns, anyone can just pass if no ideas present themselves. When all have passed, the voting can commence.
8. Encourage humor, fantasy, imagination, free flow of ideas and thoughts, etc. Brainstorming is no place for reality. Make it fun.
9. Encourage any of the following; combine, resequence/rearrange, simplify, expand, magnify, maximize/minimize, reverse, adapt, modify, substitute.
10. Break a complex problem into its component parts.
11. Allow for incubation ("sleep on it").
12. Set no time limit, if possible.
13. Encourage "cross fertilization" — the combining or adapting of others' ideas.

NONMANUFACTURING SPC

With manufacturing, it is fairly easy to determine where to put a control chart. At first, just investigate each inspection point and consider putting a control chart there. Then look for other promising spots. These should be fairly easily identified by examining the work order and flow chart. There are, of course, some exceptions to this, but they are fairly rare. Such is not the case with nonmanufacturing processes. It is almost never obvious where the charts should go, and it usually takes a great deal of knowlege about what is going on to find out. In this case, a list of possible nonmanufacturing type processes can be very helpful.

It's usual for new practitioners to be uncertain as to how to apply SPC control charts. A complete understanding of chart theory and construction, a knowledge of the types of processes used, and some actual use of the charts (some actual experience) is about the only way for a new practitioner to gain insight into how to apply the charts. This is even more true of nonmanufacturing activities (the nonmanufacturing sections of a manufacturing firm as well as a totally service firm with no manufacturing at all).

Any of the charts explained in Chapters 4 and 5 can be used in nonmanufacturing in exactly the same way as they are used in manufacturing. There are, however, three differences between manufacturing and nonmanufacturing control charts. The first one is the type of process, which emphasizes the need for the SPC practitioner to become very familiar with the processes, as well as with the charts (in other words, study hard).

The second difference for nonmanufacturing is the closer ties with the customer. Even though SPC (actually the entire SPC/TQM quality system) emphasizes closer customer considerations (for all), it is still true that most manufacturing activities can proceed to a great extent without even thinking of the customer. This is not true of most nonmanufacturing procedures. Most of these have a direct interaction with the customer. Customer needs and expectations must be more clearly identified and then translated into product and service goals. The customer must be able to see that the procedures are being made simpler, that quality control and improvement methods are being implemented, and that many activities (those that cost money, as well as such things as customer waiting time) are being reduced to their absolute limit.

The third difference is the use of a day's production as a sample. This occurs frequently in nonmanufacturing (as it does in production with long manufacturing times). In this situation, it is often best to do a 100% inspection of each day's production (or whatever is produced that day) and to then use that day's production as if it were a subgroup (all samples, or subgroups, are inspected 100%, of course). Actually, this makes no difference as far as the chart is concerned, because the chart construction of Chapter 5 and the analysis procedures of Chapter 6 can still be used as explained. This paragraph only refers to attributes charts (Chapter 5) — and then usually only average *p* charts. If the characteristic is to be measured, the regular charts of Chapter 4 can be used.

Following are some examples of types of nonmanufacturing processes (a checklist of possibilities). Customers, internal surveys, and teams and brainstorming can all be quite helpful in determining which processes need to be studied, that is, which can best profit from a quality analysis.

1. Paperwork processing — volume, CRT, etc.
2. Dollar savings.
3. Cost of quality.
4. Quality ratings.
5. Productivity.
6. Sales — type, amount, distance, etc.
7. Receivables — dollars paid in 30, 60, 90 days, dollars paid over a certain dollar amount; percent don't pay; percent don't deliver; percent contaminants; percent moisture; etc.
8. Payables — time, amount behind, etc.
9. Man-hours.
10. Line items per man-hour.
11. Documents per man-hour.
12. Boxes, etc., per man-hour.

13. Receptionist. Call randomly and rate response. Rate things such as: number of rings after 5, courtesy, no answer, on hold more than 2 minutes, disconnect, transfer to wrong party, etc.
14. Volume of activity.
15. Cycle time; timeliness.
16. Customer goals — quality improvement program, waiting time, quality of products, courtesy, timeliness, etc.
17. Perceptions of quality (internal and external).
18. Peer review and self-assessment (especially for programmers, writers, managers, engineers, etc.).
19. Correspondence — substantive errors, errors of content, typos, misspellings, timeliness, lost work, etc.
20. Issuing or storing to inventory — errors (accuracy), organization, charts for different aisles, weighted as to aisles, ease of finding, etc.
21. Quality instead of quantity.
22. Purchasing — quality and amount of product or service; rating of suppliers; quality in job performance; cost reduction (quantity and dollar amount - composite weighted index); dollar amount of purchase orders processed; reduction of supply base (reduction of suppliers); improvement results by teams, individuals, and/or departments (weighted scale, usually).

— Chapter 8 —

ACCEPTANCE SAMPLING

The inspection of incoming material is known as acceptance sampling. It can be used in most instances except for special cases where 100% inspection is absolutely necessary. Most acceptance sampling plans are based on MIL-STD-105E (MIL-STD stands for Military Standard; the plan was devised by the U.S. Government and it has been widely adopted by industry). An explanation of the most important, and most used, portion of this plan will be presented in this chapter. In order to understand the basis for this standard, it is first necessary to have some grounding in the basic probability rules, the Poisson probability distribution, and the most used sampling plan criteria.

Except for MIL-STD-105E, much of the information in this chapter is presented more for understanding than for actual use. The reader will not be expected to use the information in this chapter to actually construct a sampling plan. In fact, sampling plans have already been constructed for almost every conceivable use, so inventing a new one is probably not necessary.

PROBABILITY RULES

Probability is quite simply the chance that something will happen. It is quantified in terms of a ratio: a value divided into part of that value. For instance, in a situation where there are a total of 100 errors shared by many workers, and one worker has 5 of those errors, then the probability that that person's next action will be an error is 5/100 (0.05 or 5%).

The symbol *P* represents the probability that an event will occur, and

1 - P is the probability that it will not occur. Usually, the symbol P is associated with a letter or number to show the type or kind of event. Thus $P(\mathrm{E})$ or P_{E} usually means the probability of an event, but any other letter or number can also be substituted (such as P_{A} or P_1) depending on the best way to keep track of the events. The symbol for a success (or failure, whichever is being measured) is s, and the symbol for the total number in the sample is n. (Since the relevant event in quality control is a failure, s usually represents a failure in quality control.) In a probability problem statement, an "or" can mean either plus (+) or minus (-), and an "and" means to multiply (×). These words ("and" or "or") are sometimes missing in a statement, but they are always implied in the nature of the problem (if all the words in a statement were applied precisely, the "ands" and the "ors" would be there). This emphasizes the need to be careful in analyzing the nature of a problem — an understanding of language is obviously important.

The basic formula for computing a probability value is:

$$P(\mathrm{E}) = P_{\mathrm{E}} = s/n.$$

This means that the probability of an event is the number of these events divided by the number of times it is possible for these events to occur.

For instance, the probability that a coin flipped once will land on its "head" is $^1/_2$. Since there is only one head and only two possible positions (ignoring the infinitesimal possibility that the coin will land on its edge), $s = 1$ and $n = 2$. Therefore, $P(\mathrm{Event}) = P_{\mathrm{E}} = P(\mathrm{Head}) = P_{\mathrm{H}} = s/n = {}^1/_2$. If the coin were to be flipped twice, the probability that there would be one head is: $P(\mathrm{Head}) = P(\mathrm{Head\ and\ Tail})$ or $P(\mathrm{Tail\ and\ Head}) = [P_{\mathrm{H}} \times P_{\mathrm{T}}] + [P_{\mathrm{T}} \times P_{\mathrm{H}}] = [^1/_2 \times {}^1/_2] + [^1/_2 \times {}^1/_2] = {}^2/_4 = {}^1/_2$. Notice that neither the "and" nor the "or" were stated in this problem, but they were implied in the logic. (If the problem had been stated meticulously, the "ands" and the "ors" would have been there, and it could have been stated as, "what is the probability of a head *and* a tail *or* a tail *and* a head.")

There are several aspects of probability called fundamental properties. First, all events lie between 0 and 1 (or between 0 and 100%). Second, zero (0) or 0% is the probability that an event will never occur, while one (1) or 100% is the probability that it will always occur. Third, the sum of all probabilities of a situation will equal one (1.00...) or 100%. For instance, the sum of all probabilities for the event "rolling a die" is $^1/_6 + {}^1/_6 + {}^1/_6 + {}^1/_6 + {}^1/_6 + {}^1/_6 = {}^6/_6 = 1$. Fourth, the sum of the probability of an event occurring and of its not occurring is equal to one ($P_{\mathrm{E}} + [1 - P_{\mathrm{E}}] = 1$). Fifth, the probability that an event will occur is equal to 1 minus the probability that it will not (and vice versa). For instance, the probability that a die will show a one (1) is 1 in 6, or $^1/_6$, so the probability that it will not show a one (1) is $1 - {}^1/_6$, or $^5/_6$. This property is called the complementary rule. Note how all of these properties are interrelated, and how each follows (can be derived from) the others.

The Combination Rule

There are essentially two probability rules, and each one has an important corollary, or special case. They are the combination rule and the conditional rule. The combination rule is used to find the probability of an event if one or both of two events is operating. The equation is:

$P(A \text{ or } B \text{ or both}) = P(A) + P(B) - P(A \text{ and } B).$

In other words, this is the probability that A is true, or B is true, or both are true. Note that the "or" in the statement is either addition or subtraction. The "and" in the third term can refer to a multiplication if all groups are equal (such as: there are always 4 suits and 13 cards in a suit in a deck of 52 playing cards). However, this equality very rarely happens in real life. Therefore, logic must be used to find the probability of the third, or subtracted, term. Two examples will be used to illustrate this.

Example 8.1.

Find the probability of getting a jack or a club on one draw from a complete deck of 52 playing cards.

$P(J \text{ or } C) = P(J) + P(C) - P(J \text{ and } C) = {}^{4}/_{52} + {}^{13}/_{52} - {}^{1}/_{52} = {}^{16}/_{52}.$

The first term (${}^{4}/_{52}$) represents the 4 jacks and the second term (${}^{13}/_{52}$) the 13 clubs. The third term (${}^{1}/_{52}$), the probability of a jack and a club, is subtracted because the probability of a jack of clubs will otherwise be included twice, once in the first term and once in the second. Since there is only one way of drawing one card and getting both a jack and a club, the third term can be deduced from logic using the fundamental properties. Each card has the probability of being chosen once in every 52 trials. Therefore, the probability that a jack of clubs will be drawn is $s/n = {}^{1}/_{52}$. In this case, because all groups are equal (4 of each kind of card and 13 in each suit), the third term could have been derived by multiplying (${}^{4}/_{52} \times {}^{13}/_{52} = 52/(52 \times 52) = {}^{1}/_{52}$). However, since this seldom happens in real life, it is best to use logic and the fundamental properties in finding the probability of the subtracted term.

Example 8.2.

A box contains 50 colored and numbered balls. There are 20 green balls numbered from 1 to 20; 10 yellow balls numbered from 1 to 10; 12 red balls numbered from 1 to 12; and 8 blue balls numbered from 1 to 8. What is the probability that one ball drawn from the box will be a green ball or be numbered 10?

$$P(G \text{ or } 10) = P(G) + P(10) - P(G \text{ and } 10) = {}^{20}/_{50} + {}^{3}/_{50} - {}^{1}/_{50} = {}^{22}/_{50}.$$

In the first term (${}^{20}/_{50}$), there are 20 green balls out of 50. In the second term (${}^{3}/_{50}$), there are only 3 balls numbered 10 (there is no blue ball numbered 10). In the third term (${}^{1}/_{50}$), there is 1 green ball numbered 10. Since a green ball numbered 10 is included twice (once in the first term and once in the second), the probability of 1 green ball out of 50 (${}^{1}/_{50}$) must be subtracted. In this problem, because the groups are not equal, there is no possibility of multiplying within the third term.

If *A* and *B* are mutually exclusive, there can be no third term. This is a special case of the combination rule (often called the additive rule). Mutually exclusive means that the occurrence of one event makes the other event impossible (this would be true, for instance, if the probability in Example 8.2 above was for a blue ball numbered 10). In this case, the formula would be the same except that the third term (the subtracted term) would be missing [the $P(B \text{ or } 10) = P(B) + P(10)$].

The Conditional Rule

The second probability rule is called the conditional rule. This is the probability that two events will occur (or not occur, depending on what is wanted). The formula is:

$$P(A \text{ and } B) = P(A) \times P(B/A).$$

This means that the probability that both event *A* and event *B* will occur is the product of the probability of *A* and the probability of *B* given that *A* has already occurred. Notice that an "and" appears in this formula. An "and" in the statement means multiply (×).

Example 8.3.

A box contains 50 parts, with 5 of them defective. If two parts are randomly drawn and inspected, what is the probability that both will be defective? Assume that the first part was not replaced before the second was drawn. Once again, notice that an "and" does not appear in the statement and must, therefore, be implied in the logic (the statement could have been "what is the probability that *A and B* will be defective if neither were replaced?").

$$P(A \text{ and } B) = P(A) \times P(B/A) = {}^{5}/_{50} \times {}^{4}/_{49} = {}^{20}/_{2450}, \text{ or } {}^{1}/_{122.5}.$$

On the first draw, there were 5 defectives available out of a total of 50 parts, and a defective part was chosen. On the second, there were only 4 defective parts left and 49 total parts. This is a case where the probability of the second draw was clearly dependent on the first draw, and illustrates the importance of the statistical concept of "independence."

If the first unit had been replaced before the second unit was drawn, the probabilities would have been "independent." When the probabilities are independent, the $P(B/A)$ degenerates into $P(B)$ only, and the formula is: $P(A \text{ and } B) = P(A) \times P(B)$. In this form, the rule is called the multiplicative, or product, rule. The answer to this problem, then, when the two draws are independent (the units are replaced), is

$$P(A \text{ and } B) = P(A) \times P(B) = {}^{5}/_{50} \times {}^{5}/_{50} = {}^{25}/_{2500}, \text{ or } {}^{1}/_{100}.$$

Notice that the probability, when the units are "independent," is less than the probability when the units are "dependent." This almost always occurs.

COUNTING RULES

It is very important in probability to accurately determine the number of subjects in a group. Sometimes this can be done fairly easily by adding the subjects in all groups; or, if the number of subjects in each group is equal, the total can be found by multiplying the number of subjects in one group by the number of groups. At other times (and this occurs more often than not), more complex methods must be employed.

If the possible sets of objects are to be ordered (arranged in specific ways), then these sets are called permutations. A permutation is defined as an ordered arrangement of n objects taken d at a time. The equation is:

$${}_{n}P_{d} = n!/(n - d)!$$

The exclamation mark (!) means factorial. $n! = n(n-1)(n-2)....(n-n)$. $0!$ always $= 1$.

Example 8.4.

Find the permutation of 6 things taken 2 at a time.

$${}_{6}P_{2} = 6!/(6 - 2)! = (6 \times 5 \times 4 \times 3 \times 2 \times 1 \times 1)/(4 \times 3 \times 2 \times 1 \times 1) = 30.$$

If the way that the objects are ordered is not important, the set is called a combination, and the equation is:

$${}_{n}C_{d} = C_{d} = \binom{n}{d} = n!/[d!(n - d)!].$$

Example 8.5.

The combination of 6 things taken two at a time is:

$${}_{6}C_{2} = \binom{6}{2} = 6! / 2!(6 - 2)! =$$
$$(6 \times 5 \times 4 \times 3 \times 2 \times 1 \times 1)/(2 \times 1 \times 1)(4 \times 3 \times 2 \times 1 \times 1) = 15.$$

The following Example 8.6 shows the practical differences between permutations and combinations.

Example 8.6.

In horse racing, there is a bet called the Trisecta where you bet on the first three horses crossing the finish line (win, place, and show). In this case, of course, the order of the finish is important. If ten horses are running, the number of possible winning combinations is the permutation of 10 things taken 3 at a time, or 720 (${}_{10}P_3 = 720$). If the order of finishing were not important (all you had to do were to name the first three horses no matter what position each one had), the number of bets needed, to cover all possibilities, is only 120 (the combination of 10 things taken 3 at a time, or ${}_{10}C_3 = 120$).

The combinations formula is used extensively in complex probability distributions, such as the binomial, hypergeometric, etc., although both permutations and combinations have real life applications (the combination is used so much in quality control because the order of failures is not important, only how many). In fact, it is possible to derive most distribution formulas using the simple probability and counting rules, although it is usually not done this way.

THE POISSON DISTRIBUTION

The hypergeometric, the binomial, the Poisson, and the Student's t distributions (as well as the normal — see Chapter 3) have important applications in quality control. However, the Poisson can be used in place of the others for most acceptance sampling applications as long as certain rules are obeyed (such is also the case for control charts, where the normal is used in place of other distributions).

The Poisson formula is what is called a single term formula, and it gives the probability of exactly c number of defects (the c in the Poisson refers to the number of defects, and means exactly the same thing that d means in permutations and combinations). The equation is:

$$P(c) = e^{-np} (np)^c / c!$$

where

$P(c)$ = the probability of c defects or failures
c = the number of acceptable defects, or events
p = the fraction defective (as in the p chart)
n = the sample size
np = the average number of defects
e = the base of Napierian (natural) logarithms = 2.71828....

If the probability of more than, or less than, c defects is desired, more than one term must be calculated. For instance, for the probability of 1 or less defects, two terms must be calculated and added together — one with $c = 0$ and one with $c = 1$ (notice how the additive rule is used here; $P_0 + P_1$). To find the probability of more than 1 defect, calculate the probability of 0 and the probability of 1, add together, and subtract from 1. (In this case, the complementary rule is also used.)

Theoretically, the Poisson can have an infinite number of terms, representing an infinite number of defects (nonconformities). The sum of the probabilities of all of these conditions must equal 1.00, or 100%, even though the number of these conditions is unknown, or infinite (the Poisson can also be used when the sample size is known, or finite).

Poisson expansions must begin with $c = 0$ (for zero defects).

The calculation of the Poisson terms is tedious and time consuming (and sometimes impossible) when many terms are involved — such as the probability of five or more [P(5 or more)]. Therefore, the Poisson tables have been prepared to overcome this problem; they are found in Table 3 at the back of the book. The tables are quite easy to use, which is one of the reasons that the Poisson has found such a wide application in so many fields. As the Poisson is expanded to more and more terms, the probabilities quickly become very small. For this reason, the Poisson tables provide the probabilities of only a limited number of Poisson terms (to three places). When the probabilities get so small that the first three decimal places are zeros, the table ends.

As was explained above in the section on probability rules, it is essential to understand precisely what is needed, or asked for. Therefore, a knowledge of language is critical. For instance, the statement can ask for the probability of more than 2, or 2 or more, or less than 2, or 2 or less, etc. Each is a different statement and must be handled differently. For instance, it will be noted that the probability of more than 2 means the same thing as the probability of 3 or more, and the probability of 2 or more means the same thing as the probability of more than 1. Since the Poisson tables only go one way, it is necessary to change the way the problem is stated to reflect this.

To use the tables, two values are needed: np which is found in the left-hand column, and c which is across the top. The body of the table is a probability value and is cumulative; it is an "or less than" value. The additive and complementary rules of probability are especially useful in using these tables. Some examples will be quite useful in developing an understanding as to how the tables are used. Another example is the one shown in the section of this chapter entitled "Sampling Plan Design."

Example 8.7.

Use np = 2 and the Poisson tables to find the following probability values.

> P(2 or less) = 0.677. Use the tables direct.
> P(2) = P(2 or less) - P(1 or less) = 0.677 - 0.406 = 0.271.
> P(more than 2) = 1 - P(2 or less) = 1 - 0.677 = 0.323.
> P(2 or more) = 1 - P(1 or less) = 1 - 0.406 = 0.594.
> P(less than 2) = P(1 or less) = 0.406.

SAMPLING PLAN DEFINITION

A sampling plan is, essentially, the number of pieces to be inspected, n, and the number of acceptable defectives, A (Ac in MIL-STD-105E), and the number of unacceptable defectives, R (Re in MIL-STD-105E). Frequently a lot size, N, is also shown because there is some relationship between lot size and sample size (a good sample plan will have n at or less than 10% of N). In simple plans the reject number, R, is always just 1 more than A, and therefore does not need to be shown (however, it is shown in MIL-STD-105E).

The sampling plan of N = 800, n = 70, A = 1, and R = 2 means: choose a random sample of 70 units from the lot of 800 and inspect the characteristic (compare it to a standard or specification). If there is only 1 or less defective part that does not meet the standards or the specification, accept the entire lot of 800. If there are 2 or more, reject the lot.

Some plans show a gap between A and R, such as: N = 800, n = 50, A = 1, and R = 3. This plan is similar to the other except that a separate decision is required when the number of defects equals 2. This type of plan occurs, for instance, when a reduced sampling plan is used (as above, where only 50 units are sampled rather than 70). If a sample from this type of plan were to have 2 defectives, the lot of 800 would be accepted, but the next lot, from the same vendor or machine, would be returned to regular inspection (where n = 70 rather than 50, and R = 2 rather than 3).

Sampling plans can also require multiple samples. The plan N = 800, n_1 = 45, n_2 = 45, A_1 = 0, A_2 = 2, R_1 = 2, and R_2 = 3 means: take a random sample of 45 from the lot and measure the applicable characteristic. If no defectives are found, accept the lot. If 1 or 2 defectives are found, take a second sample of 45 and measure. If the total number of defects from both samples (from the full 90 units measured) is 2 or less, accept; otherwise reject. Multiple sampling plans have been devised for as many as 7 successive samples.

The advantage of this type of plan (multiple sampling) is that vendors with very good lots have their lots almost always accepted on the first sample, with smaller samples and lower costs (very bad lots are also rejected on the first sample). Unfortunately, medium quality lots would be more expensive to inspect (90 units instead of 70) and so this plan could be a disadvantage for some vendors. There is also a psychological advantage to multiple sampling plans in that they appear to give a second chance for acceptance. Actually, the probability of acceptance is the same whether a single or a multiple plan is used.

LOT SIZE AND DISPOSITION

Lot size and organization is dependent on many factors including part size and configuration, material handling methods, consumer's plant dynamics, transportation and delivery methods, packaging, and economic quantities. Lots should be organized to facilitate sampling procedures (buyers should require vendors to do this). The best sampling procedure is one that allows for the best and cheapest handling and assures total randomness (an unbiased sample).

A sampling procedure can be a simple sample that takes a sample of 150 from a lot of 3,000 at random through the entire lot, or it can be stratified (called stratified random sampling). In stratified sampling, layers are first picked at random after which several units are picked at random from each chosen layer (rows and columns can also be chosen in this way).

When a sample fails to meet the sampling plan criteria (the percent defective is too high), the lot is considered unacceptable and some disposition must be made of the lot. One of three methods can be used. First, the lot can be accepted and sent to production. Second, the lot can be rectified at the consumer's plant, by the consumer's own inspectors (usually 100% inspection). These first two methods are considered unacceptable in most firms today (except in cases where the parts are needed desperately). Third, lots can be returned to the vendor for rectification. This is considered the best of the three because the extra cost and trouble become the vendor's responsibility, and the vendor is directly involved in the rectification process (this gives a powerful motivation for the vendors to improve their quality). Rectified lots are not inspected again at the buyer's plant.

SAMPLING PLAN DESIGN

In order to design a sampling plan, four values must be known: producer's risk (α or alpha), consumer's risk (β or beta), acceptable quality level (AQL), and lot tolerance percent defective (LTPD). These values are usually determined from past experience, engineering estimate, management decisions, mathematical calculation, and/or specified by the buyer as part of the contract. For instance, suppose that the consumer has learned by experience that a lot with more than 9% defective product will disrupt the consumer's plant. This, then, becomes the LTPD (LTPD = 9%, or 0.09). Suppose further (through experience) that the plant can handle up to 10% of these kinds of lots without too much chaos ($\alpha = 10\%$, or 0.10). However, if the producer were to manufacture his lots to 9% defective (that is, if his lots were to contain an average of 9% defective parts), half of them would be more than 9% defective and so rejected by the consumer. He must, therefore, manufacture to considerably less than 9% to keep many of his lots from being rejected. Suppose further that the producer wishes no more than 5% of his lots to be rejected. This 5% then becomes the producer's AQL (AQL = 5% = 0.05). An alpha value, α, can now be calculated for the producer using these three values and the Poisson distribution (the procedure is rather complicated). It is obvious from this discussion that these four values are highly interrelated.

Producer's risk (α — the Greek letter alpha) is defined as the probability that a good lot will be rejected. In calculating sampling plans, this value (α) is always subtracted from 1 to get the probability of acceptance (since probability plan calculations all use the probability of acceptance rather than rejection). In any sampling plan, there is always the possibility that an error can be made — that the percentage of defectives in the sample will be more, or less, than the percentage of defectives in the lot. The producer's risk, α, is one of those error possibilities. It is called a type I error in quality control and is defined as the rejection of an acceptable lot. This is an unnecessary cost (if only the facts were known) to the producer — hence, "producer's risk."

Acceptable quality level (AQL) is the acceptable percent defective product in a producer's lot. It is always associated with the producer's risk, α.

Consumer's risk (β — the Greek letter beta) is the probability that a "bad" lot will be accepted. Since this is already a probability of acceptance, it does not have to be subtracted from 1. Bad lots, with high amounts of defective parts, can be quite expensive to a consumer. If a bad lot gets past the inspection process, it can cause a great deal of trouble in the consumer's plant (rework, shutdowns, etc.). This is another type of mistake a sampling plan can make and is called a type II error in quality control (accepting a bad lot). Since this type of mistake increases costs to the consumer, it is called consumer's risk.

The Lot Tolerance Percent Defective LTPD (also known as "Limiting Quality Level," or LQL) is the maximum fraction defective that can be tolerated by a consumer. It is always associated with consumer's risk, β.

Once the AQL, α, LTPD, and β are known, a sampling plan can be calculated using the inverse of the Poisson probability distribution (while other distributions may be required for some plans, the Poisson applies almost universally and is the easiest to use). Only the sample number n and the acceptance number A (called c in the Poisson) are calculated for simple plans. Calculations for multiple sampling plans are similar, except that the probability values are calculated from complex formulas rather than simply lifting a number from a table. The rejection number R does not need to be calculated for single sampling plans as it is always 1 more than the acceptance number A (c in the Poisson).

Several iterations are necessary in the procedure, starting at A = c = 0 and continuing through A = c = 1, A = c = 2, etc., until the two sample sizes are equal, or close to it. Actually the iterations stop when the producer's sample size is either the same as the consumer's (almost never occurs) or gets larger than the consumer's (after this, the samples just get further and further apart). At the point where the producer's sample size gets larger (if they are not equal, that is), one of four plans must be chosen (if the sample sizes are equal, only one of two plans need to be chosen).

1. The plan with the smallest sample size (lowest cost). In Example 8.8, this is n = 29, A = c = 1.

2. The plan with the largest sample size (most protection). In Example 8.8, this is n = 68, A = c = 2.

3. The plan that exactly meets the producer's stipulation and also comes as close as possible to the consumer's. In Example 8.8, there are two plans that exactly meet the producer's stipulation: n = 29, A = 1; and n = 68, A = 2. To find out which of these two to use, divide the consumer's np value ($n_C p_C$) at that A value by the producer's sample size (n_P) at that A value (since this is the sample size that will be used). At n = 29, $n_C p_C / n_P$ = 3.89/29 = 0.134. At n = 68, $n_C p_C / n_P$ = 5.33/68 = 0.078. Therefore, use n = 68, A = c = 2 (since 0.078 is closer to the consumer's stipulation of 0.09 than is 0.134).

4. The plan that exactly meets the consumer's stipulation and also comes as close as possible to the producer's. In Example 8.8, there are two plans that exactly meet the consumer's stipulation: n = 43, A = 1 and n = 59, A = 2. To find out which of these two to use, divide the producer's np ($n_P p_P$) at that A value by the consumer's sample size (n_C) at that A value (since this is the sample size that will be used). At n = 43, $n_P p_P / n_C$ = 0.3458/43 = 0.008. At n = 59, $n_P p_P / n_C$ = 0.8188/59 = 0.0139. Therefore, use n = 59, A = c = 2 (since 0.0139 is closer to the producer's stipulation of 0.012 than is 0.0089).

Example 8.8.

The following values for AQL, α, LTPD, and β will now be used to illustrate the procedures.

AQL = 1.2% = 0.012 = p_P;
LTPD = 9.0 = 0.09 = p_C;
α = 5%; 1 - α = 0.95;
β = 10% = 0.10.

First Trial (A = c = 0)

$n_P p_P$ = 0.0516 (using the Poisson tables at a P of 0.95 and a c of 0, and interpolating);

$n_P = n_P p_P / p_P$ = 0.0516/0.012= 4 units;

$n_C p_C$ = 2.3 (using the Poisson tables at a P of 0.10 and a c of 0, and interpolating);

$n_C = n_C p_C / p_C$ = 2.3/0.09 = 26 units.

The two n's (4 and 26) are not equal; try c = 1.

Second Trial (A = c = 1)

$n_P p_P$ = 0.3458;

n_P = 0.3458/0.012 = 29 units;

$n_C p_C$ = 3.89;

n_C = 3.89/0.09 = 43 units;

The two n's (29 and 43) are not equal; try c = 2.

Third Trial (A = c = 2)

$n_P p_P$ = 0.8188;

n_P = 0.8188/0.012 = 68 units;

$n_C p_C$ = 5.33;

n_C = 5.33/0.09 = 59 units.

At this point, no more calculations are needed. Notice that, in trial 3, the n's switched and the consumer's sample size, n_C, became smaller than the producer's sample size, n_P. This trend will now continue forever, with greater and greater divergence for each higher c value.

OPERATING CHARACTERISTIC CURVE

The operating characteristic curve (OC Curve) can be used to evaluate quality sampling plans by finding the probability that a lot of a certain fraction defective (p) will be accepted (P_A) or rejected (1 - P_A), or finding what the fraction defective (p) must be for a certain probability of acceptance (P_A, or 1 - P_R) given a particular sampling plan. The probability that a lot will be accepted (either 1 - α or β) can be determined by finding the percent defective for the lot (either AQL or LTPD) on the abscissa (X-axis), moving up to the curve and then left to the ordinate (Y-axis), and then reading the percent from the scale on the ordinate. The maximum acceptable percent defective in a lot (either AQL or LTPD) can also be determined by finding the percent of lots acceptable (either 1 - α or β) on the ordinate axis, moving to the right to the curve and then down to the abscissa and then reading the percent from the scale on the abscissa (see Figure 8.1). The ordinate axis is the probability that a lot of given fraction defective (p) found on the abscissa will be accepted (P_A). The probability that the lot will be rejected (P_R) is 1 - P_A (1 minus the probability of accepting the lot).

These probabilities can also be calculated from the Poisson probability distribution. Suppose that the sampling plan is $n = 68$, A = 2. If a lot has no more than 1.2% (0.012) defective (or comes from a process that normally runs no more than 1.2% defective — the process average is normally about 1.2%), the probability that it will be accepted is 95%. The math is: $p = 0.012$, $n = 68$, $np = 68 \times 0.012 = 0.816$; $P_A = 0.95$ (from the Poisson tables at $np = 0.816$ and $A = c = 2$).

Conversely, for a probability of acceptance of 90%, a lot with a sampling plan of $n = 68$ and A = 2 will have no more than 1.62% defective product (or come from a process that normally runs no more than 1.62% defective product — the process average is no more than 1.62%). The math is: at $c = 2$ and $P_A = 0.90$ (900 in the tables) $np = 1.1$. $np/n = 1.1/68 = 0.0162$, or 1.62% ($p = 1.62\%$). For an 80% acceptance level (80% of the lots are accepted), the process average only needs to be about 2.226% (1.535/68).

The graph in Figure 8.1 shows an AQL of 0.012 (1.2%) at a producer's risk (α) of 0.05 (5%), and an LTPD of 0.09 (9%) at a consumer's risk (β) of 0.10 (10%). Of course, the calculations give the precise value, while reading from the graph is only approximate.

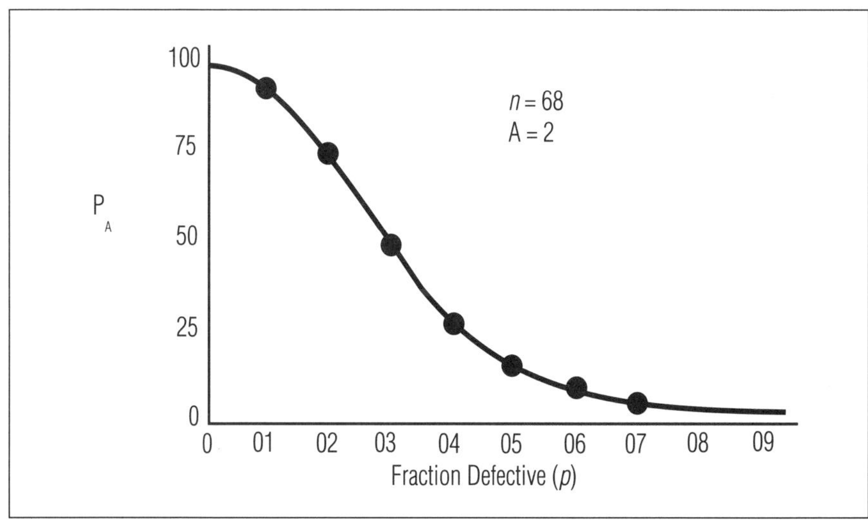

Figure 8.1. Operating characteristic curve (OC Curve).

Example 8.9.

Construct an OC curve given $n = 68$ and A = 2. First, construct a table of p and P_A by assuming seven p's and then calculating the P_A's. Then construct a curve (Figure 8.1) by graphing the P_A's and the p's. Using the first P_A value of 0.968 as an example, first multiply 0.01 by 68 to get 0.68. Then find

0.968 in the table under $c = 2$ and across from $np = 0.68$ (it will be necessary to extrapolate). The other six P_A values are found the same way.

1. $p = 0.01$, $np = 0.68$; $P_A = 0.968$
2. $p = 0.02$, $np = 1.36$; $P_A = 0.843$
3. $p = 0.03$, $np = 2.04$; $P_A = 0.666$
4. $p = 0.04$, $np = 2.72$; $P_A = 0.489$
5. $p = 0.05$, $np = 3.40$; $P_A = 0.340$
6. $p = 0.06$, $np = 4.08$; $P_A = 0.227$
7. $p = 0.07$, $np = 4.76$; $P_A = 0.147$

AOQ AND AOQL

The average outgoing quality curve (AOQ Curve) can be used to evaluate a quality sampling plan by showing the average quality accepted into the consumer's production operation from the producer (actually from the consumer's own receiving inspection) for a particular sampling plan. The OC curve only shows the percent bad product received by the customer's receiving inspection before it is rectified by 100% inspection, while the AOQ curve shows the average percent bad product received into the customer's production operation after all rejected lots have been 100% inspected. In Figure 8.2, the average quality going into the consumer's plant (accepted, or outgoing, from receiving inspection) from sampling plan n = 68 and A = 2, and for a fraction defective of 0.02 (2%), is 1.686%. In other words, for this plan (n = 68, A = 2), the consumer can expect about 1.7% bad product in his plant if the producer normally sends lots of about 2% defective.

This can also be determined mathematically. Note that 84.3% of these lots will be accepted with an average of 2% defectives ($P_A = 0.843$ at $np = 1.36$ and $A = c = 2$), while the remainder (15.7%) will be rectified. Rectified lots are rejected lots returned to the vendor for 100% inspection. Rectified lots, therefore, have 100% quality (no defectives, or $p = 0$) when returned to the customer. The calculations, then, for a p of 2%, are: $(0.843 \times 0.02) + (0.157 \times 0) = 1.686$. (Of course, 0.157×0, the outgoing quality of the rectified lots, can be dropped from the calculations.) Note that at 6%, the AOQ reduces to 1.362%, because so many lots are being rectified by the producer (of course, this presents other, often enormous, quality problems).

Actually, the only difference between the OC curve and the AOQ curve is that the OC curve shows the percent of failures delivered to the customer, while the AOQ curve shows the percent failures delivered to the customer's production operation after rectification (after 100% inspection of rejected lots). Because of this, AOQ curves are constructed by adding one column to the OC curve calculations ($AOQ = P_A \times 100p$). Note that the AOQ (see Example 8.10) is always presented as a percentage — it could, of course, be shown as a fraction defective by simply omitting the $100 \times p$ calculation and using $P_A \times p$ instead. Once again, the mathematical calculations are much more precise than simply picking a value from a graph. However, picking a value from a graph is considerably easier.

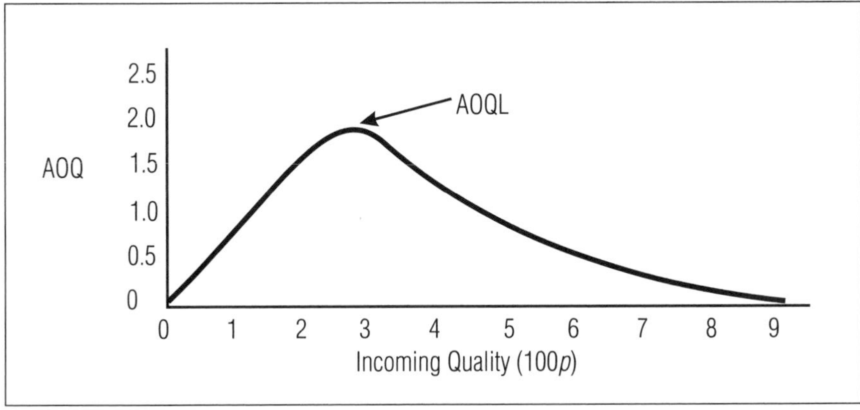

Figure 8.2. Average outgoing quality curve (AOQ Curve) for $n = 68$ and A = 2.

Example 8.10.

Construct an AOQ curve for the sampling plan $n = 68$ and A = 2. Note that the first 3 columns in the calculation table are identical to those in Example 8.9. Then construct a curve (Figure 8.2) by graphing the AOQ's and the p's (use a percentage, $100p$ instead of just p).

p	np	P_A	AOQ ($P_A \times 100p$)
0.01	0.68	0.968	0.968
0.02	1.36	0.843	1.686
0.03	2.04	0.668	2.004
0.04	2.72	0.489	1.956
0.05	3.40	0.340	1.700
0.06	4.08	0.227	1.362
0.07	4.76	0.127	0.889

Another important value — the average outgoing quality limit (AOQL) — is just the maximum of the AOQ curve. It represents the maximum possible percent defective for the sampling plan (assuming rectification of rejected lots). AOQL values can be calculated by using successive approximations around the point where the AOQ reduces (use closer and closer p values until a value is reached on both sides that does not change for a satisfactory number of decimal places — probably 3 or 4 decimal places). For the plan of Example 8.10, this occurs somewhere between 3 and 4% (successive calculations would also have to be done for p's between 2 and 3% in order to be sure just where the curve tops out).

MIL-STD-105E

MIL-STD-105E is an attributes acceptance sampling plan that indexes on the AQL. In other words, it basically matches the producer's stipulation (AQL) and comes as close as possible to the consumer's (LTPD). Alpha (α) and beta (β) are not fixed in the plan — they are not set at 0.05 and 0.10, respectively, as many think. Instead they fluctuate between 0.001 and 0.15 — although most are at, or close to, an AQL of 0.05 and an LTPD of 0.10. The plan is quite extensive and takes an entire volume of tables, graphs (OC curves, etc.), and explanations.

Three types of sampling are provided in the standard: single, double, and multiple (up to 7 samples). Each of these three types, in turn, is divided into normal, tightened, and reduced inspection. The standard is very specific about how and when these different types of plans are to be used. Tightened inspection provides greater sampling protection and is used when the supplier's quality begins to deteriorate. Reduced inspection can be used when the supplier's quality has remained excellent for a period of time. Although reduced inspection does not provide quite the protection that the other two do, it is less costly (reduced inspection is not used much, and is not included here). Tightened inspection is the costliest of all the plans.

Example 8.11.

Using the following values, determine the sampling plan from MIL-STD-105E. The AQL = 1%, the lot size = 700, the inspection level = II. Use normal inspection.

1. The first step is to determine the sampling size code letter. From Table 8.1, which reproduces part of a table from MIL-STD-105E, the code letter for a sample size of 700 (501 to 1200) and an inspection level of II is "J."

Table 8.1 Sample Size Code Letters (Extracted from MIL-STD-105E)

Lot Size	General Inspection Levels		
	I	II	III
to 8	A	A	B
15	A	B	C
25	B	C	D
50	C	D	E
90	C	E	F
150	D	F	G
280	E	G	H
500	F	H	J
1,200	G	J	K
3,200	H	K	L
10,000	J	L	M
35,000	K	M	N
150,000	L	N	P
500,000	M	P	Q
>500,000	N	Q	R

2. The next step is to read the sample plan from Table 8.2. Enter the table, from the left, at row "J." Moving to the right, the first column gives the sample size n at 80. Now move to the right to the column headed 1.0. This is an AQL of 1% (the table uses percentages rather than fraction defective). This column has two values — the acceptance number Ac and the rejection number Re. In normal inspection, the rejection number is always one more than the acceptance number. The plan is then: N = 700, n = 80, Ac = 2, Re = 3.

In the event that an arrow appears in the Ac/Re column, follow the arrow (either up or down) and use the plan that the arrow points to. For instance, the sampling plan to be used for a code letter of F and an AQL of 0.40% is: n = 32, A = 0, R = 1 (not n = 20, A = 0, R = 1). Double and multiple tables, and tightened and reduced, can be read in the same way.

The table can also be used for defects per unit by using the columns headed 1.0 to 1000 (this is still an AQL). In this case, the numbers are defects per unit, not percentages (actually, the numbers 1.0 to 100 can be either percentages of defectives or defects per unit, although no one could possibly want a large percentage of defectives).

The plan just described for normal inspection would move to tightened inspection if 2 out of any 5 consecutive lots are rejected (none of these can be rectified lots). For our example plan, the requirements under tightened inspection would be (Table 8.3): N = 700, n = 80, A = 1, R = 2.

Normal inspection can be resumed only when 5 lots in a row are accepted.

Inspection level II is the normal level, for normal products. Level III has increased sample sizes and is used for expensive items where a higher level of protection is needed. Level I has a reduced sample size, and reduced protection, and is used for destructive and dangerous tests. There are other codes but they require special training to apply and are very rarely used.

Table 8.2 Single Sampling Plans for Normal Inspection

Acceptable Quality Levels

Sample size code letter	Sample size	0.010		0.015		0.025		0.040		0.065		0.10		0.15		0.25		0.40		0.65		1.0		1.5		2.5		4.0		6.5		10		15		25		40		65		100		150		250		400		650		1000	
		Ac	Re	Ac	Re	Ac	Re	Ac	Re	Ac	Re	Ac	Re	Ac	Re	Ac	Re	Ac	Re	Ac	Re	Ac	Re	Ac	Re	Ac	Re	Ac	Re	Ac	Re	Ac	Re	Ac	Re	Ac	Re	Ac	Re	Ac	Re	Ac	Re	Ac	Re	Ac	Re	Ac	Re	Ac	Re	Ac	Re
A	2	↓		↓		↓		↓		↓		↓		↓		↓		↓		↓		↓		↓		↓		↓		0	1	↓		↓		1	2	2	3	3	4	5	6	7	8	10	11	14	15	21	22	30	31
B	3	↓		↓		↓		↓		↓		↓		↓		↓		↓		↓		↓		↓		↓		0	1	↑		↓		1	2	2	3	3	4	5	6	7	8	10	11	14	15	21	22	30	31	44	45
C	5	↓		↓		↓		↓		↓		↓		↓		↓		↓		↓		↓		↓		0	1	↑		↓		1	2	2	3	3	4	5	6	7	8	10	11	14	15	21	22	30	31	44	45	↑	
D	8	↓		↓		↓		↓		↓		↓		↓		↓		↓		↓		↓		0	1	↑		↓		1	2	2	3	3	4	5	6	7	8	10	11	14	15	21	22	30	31	44	45	↑		↑	
E	13	↓		↓		↓		↓		↓		↓		↓		↓		↓		↓		0	1	↑		↓		1	2	2	3	3	4	5	6	7	8	10	11	14	15	21	22	30	31	44	45	↑		↑		↑	
F	20	↓		↓		↓		↓		↓		↓		↓		↓		↓		0	1	↑		↓		1	2	2	3	3	4	5	6	7	8	10	11	14	15	21	22	↑		↑		↑		↑		↑		↑	
G	32	↓		↓		↓		↓		↓		↓		↓		↓		0	1	↑		↓		1	2	2	3	3	4	5	6	7	8	10	11	14	15	21	22	↑		↑		↑		↑		↑		↑		↑	
H	50	↓		↓		↓		↓		↓		↓		↓		0	1	↑		↓		1	2	2	3	3	4	5	6	7	8	10	11	14	15	21	22	↑		↑		↑		↑		↑		↑		↑		↑	
J	80	↓		↓		↓		↓		↓		↓		0	1	↑		↓		1	2	2	3	3	4	5	6	7	8	10	11	14	15	21	22	↑		↑		↑		↑		↑		↑		↑		↑		↑	
K	125	↓		↓		↓		↓		↓		0	1	↑		↓		1	2	2	3	3	4	5	6	7	8	10	11	14	15	21	22	↑		↑		↑		↑		↑		↑		↑		↑		↑		↑	
L	200	↓		↓		↓		↓		0	1	↑		↓		1	2	2	3	3	4	5	6	7	8	10	11	14	15	21	22	↑		↑		↑		↑		↑		↑		↑		↑		↑		↑		↑	
M	315	↓		↓		↓		0	1	↑		↓		1	2	2	3	3	4	5	6	7	8	10	11	14	15	21	22	↑		↑		↑		↑		↑		↑		↑		↑		↑		↑		↑		↑	
N	500	↓		↓		0	1	↑		↓		1	2	2	3	3	4	5	6	7	8	10	11	14	15	21	22	↑		↑		↑		↑		↑		↑		↑		↑		↑		↑		↑		↑		↑	
P	800	↓		0	1	↑		↓		1	2	2	3	3	4	5	6	7	8	10	11	14	15	21	22	↑		↑		↑		↑		↑		↑		↑		↑		↑		↑		↑		↑		↑		↑	
Q	1250	0	1	↑		↓		1	2	2	3	3	4	5	6	7	8	10	11	14	15	21	22	↑		↑		↑		↑		↑		↑		↑		↑		↑		↑		↑		↑		↑		↑		↑	
R	2000	↑		↑		1	2	2	3	3	4	5	6	7	8	10	11	14	15	21	22	↑		↑		↑		↑		↑		↑		↑		↑		↑		↑		↑		↑		↑		↑		↑		↑	

↓ Use first sampling plan below arrow. If sample size equals or exceeds lot or batch size, do 100% inspection.

↑ Use first sampling plan above arrow.

Ac = Acceptance number

Re = Rejection number

Table 8.3 Single Sampling Plans for Tightened Inspection

Sample size code letter	Sample size	0.010	0.015	0.025	0.040	0.065	0.10	0.15	0.25	0.40	0.65	1.0	1.5	2.5	4.0	6.5	10	15	25	40	65	100	150	250	400	650	1000
		Ac Re	Ac Re	Ac Re	Ac Re	Ac Re	Ac Re	Ac Re	Ac Re	Ac Re	Ac Re	Ac Re	Ac Re	Ac Re	Ac Re	Ac Re	Ac Re	Ac Re	Ac Re	Ac Re	Ac Re	Ac Re	Ac Re	Ac Re	Ac Re	Ac Re	Ac Re
A	2	↓	↓	↓	↓	↓	↓	↓	↓	↓	↓	↓	↓	↓	↓	↓	↓	↓	↓	1 2	2 3	3 4	5 6	8 9	12 13	18 19	27 28
B	3	↓	↓	↓	↓	↓	↓	↓	↓	↓	↓	↓	↓	↓	↓	0 1	↓	↓	1 2	2 3	3 4	5 6	8 9	12 13	18 19	27 28	41 42
C	5	↓	↓	↓	↓	↓	↓	↓	↓	↓	↓	↓	↓	↓	0 1	↓	↓	1 2	2 3	3 4	5 6	8 9	12 13	18 19	27 28	41 42	↑
D	8	↓	↓	↓	↓	↓	↓	↓	↓	↓	↓	↓	↓	0 1	↓	↓	1 2	2 3	3 4	5 6	8 9	12 13	18 19	27 28	41 42	↑	↑
E	13	↓	↓	↓	↓	↓	↓	↓	↓	↓	↓	↓	0 1	↓	↓	1 2	2 3	3 4	5 6	8 9	12 13	18 19	27 28	41 42	↑	↑	↑
F	20	↓	↓	↓	↓	↓	↓	↓	↓	↓	↓	0 1	↓	↓	1 2	2 3	3 4	5 6	8 9	12 13	18 19	↑	↑	↑	↑	↑	↑
G	32	↓	↓	↓	↓	↓	↓	↓	↓	↓	0 1	↓	↓	1 2	2 3	3 4	5 6	8 9	12 13	18 19	↑	↑	↑	↑	↑	↑	↑
H	50	↓	↓	↓	↓	↓	↓	↓	↓	0 1	↓	↓	1 2	2 3	3 4	5 6	8 9	12 13	18 19	↑	↑	↑	↑	↑	↑	↑	↑
J	80	↓	↓	↓	↓	↓	↓	↓	0 1	↓	↓	1 2	2 3	3 4	5 6	8 9	12 13	18 19	↑	↑	↑	↑	↑	↑	↑	↑	↑
K	125	↓	↓	↓	↓	↓	↓	0 1	↓	↓	1 2	2 3	3 4	5 6	8 9	12 13	18 19	↑	↑	↑	↑	↑	↑	↑	↑	↑	↑
L	200	↓	↓	↓	↓	↓	0 1	↓	↓	1 2	2 3	3 4	5 6	8 9	12 13	18 19	↑	↑	↑	↑	↑	↑	↑	↑	↑	↑	↑
M	315	↓	↓	↓	↓	0 1	↓	↓	1 2	2 3	3 4	5 6	8 9	12 13	18 19	↑	↑	↑	↑	↑	↑	↑	↑	↑	↑	↑	↑
N	500	↓	↓	↓	0 1	↓	↓	1 2	2 3	3 4	5 6	8 9	12 13	18 19	↑	↑	↑	↑	↑	↑	↑	↑	↑	↑	↑	↑	↑
P	800	↓	↓	0 1	↓	↓	1 2	2 3	3 4	5 6	8 9	12 13	18 19	↑	↑	↑	↑	↑	↑	↑	↑	↑	↑	↑	↑	↑	↑
Q	1250	↓	0 1	↓	↓	1 2	2 3	3 4	5 6	8 9	12 13	18 19	↑	↑	↑	↑	↑	↑	↑	↑	↑	↑	↑	↑	↑	↑	↑
R	2000	0 1	↑	↓	1 2	2 3	3 4	5 6	8 9	12 13	18 19	↑	↑	↑	↑	↑	↑	↑	↑	↑	↑	↑	↑	↑	↑	↑	↑
S	3150			1 2								↑	↑	↑	↑	↑	↑	↑	↑	↑	↑	↑	↑	↑	↑	↑	↑

(Column heading: Acceptable Quality Levels)

↓ Use first sampling plan below arrow. If sample size equals or exceeds lot or batch size, do 100% inspection.

↑ Use first sampling plan above arrow.

Ac = Acceptance number

Re = Rejection number

— Bibliography —

American National Standard — ANSI/ASQC Q91— 1993, American Society for Quality Control, 611 East Wisconsin Avenue, Milwaukee, WI. There are similar publications for ISO 9000 (Q90), ISO 9002 (Q92), ISO 9003 (Q93), and ISO 9004 (Q94).

An Education and Training Strategy for Total Quality Management in the Department of Defense, Office of the Assistant Secretary of Defense, (P&L) TQM/IPO, Washington, DC, 1989.

ASQC Statistics Division, *Glossary and Tables for Statistical Quality Control*, Milwaukee, WI 1983.

ASTM, *Manual on Presentation of Data and Control Chart Analysis*, Philadelphia, PA.

Atkinson, P. E., *Creating Culture Change*, San Diego, CA: Pfeiffer and Company, 1990.

Barker, T. B., *Quality by Experimental Design*, New York: Marcel Dekker, 1985.

Besterfield, D. H., *Quality Control*, 3rd Ed., Englewood Cliffs, NJ: Prentice Hall, 1991.

Bhote, K. R., *World Class Quality*, New York: AMA Publications, 1988.

Box, G. E. P., Hunter, W. G., and Hunter, J. S., *Statistics for Experimenters*, New York: Wiley, 1978.

Brassard, M., *The Memory Jogger Plus*, Methuen, MA, Goal/QPC, 1989.

Braverman, J. D., *Fundamentals of Statistical Quality Control*, Reston, VA: Reston Publishing, 1981.

Covey, S. R., *The Seven Habits of Highly Effective People*, New York: Simon and Schuster, 1989.

Crosby, P. B., *Quality is Free*, New York: McGraw-Hill, 1979.

Crosby, P. B., *Quality Without Tears*, New York: McGraw-Hill, 1984.

Deming, W. E., *Quality, Productivity and Competitive Position*, Cambridge, MA: MIT Press, 1982.

Deming, W. E., *Out of the Crisis*, Cambridge, MA: MIT Press, 1986.

Dockstader, S. L. and Houston, A., *A Total Quality Management Process Improvement Model*, San Diego, CA: Navy Personnel Research and Development Center, 1988.

Doty, L. A., *Reliability for the Technologies*, 2nd Ed., New York: Industrial Press, 1989.

Doty, L. A., *Statistical Process Control*, 2nd Ed., New York: Industrial Press, 1996.

Doty, L. A., *Work Methods and Measurement for Management*, Albany: Delmar, 1989.

Fawcett, M., *An ISO 9000 Implementation Plan*, New York: dk Press, 1993.

Feigenbaum, A. V., *Total Quality Control*, 3rd Ed., New York: McGraw-Hill, 1991.

Glasser, W., MD, *Control Theory*, New York: Harper and Row, 1984.

Glasser, W., MD, *Control Theory in the Classroom*, New York: Harper and Row, 1985.

Glasser, W., MD, *The Identity Society*, New York: Harper and Row, 1972.

Glasser, W., MD, *Schools Without Failure*, New York: Harper and Row, 1969.

Hayes, G.E. and Romig, H.G., *Modern Quality Control*, Encino, CA: Glencoe, 1982.

Herzberg, F., *The Motivation to Work*, New York: Wiley, 1959.

Hicks, C. R., *Fundamental Concepts in the Design of Experiments*, 3rd Ed., New York: Oxford University Press, 1994.

Imai, M., *Kaizen*, New York: McGraw-Hill, 1986.

Ishikawa, K., *Introduction to Quality Control*, New York: Quality Resources, 1990.

Jaehn, A., "All Purpose Charts Can Make SPC Easy," *Quality Progress*, American Society for Quality Control, Milwaukee, WI, February, 1989.

Johnson, P. L., *Keeping Score*, New York: Harper and Row, 1989.

Jones and McBride, *An Introduction to Team Approach Problem Solving*, Milwaukee, WI: ASQC Press, 1990.

Juran, J. M., *Juran on Leadership for Quality*, New York: Free Press, 1989.

Juran, J. M., *Juran on Planning for Quality*, New York: Free Press, 1988.

Juran, J. M. and Gryna, F.M., *Quality Control Handbook*, 4th Ed., New York: McGraw-Hill, 1994.

Juran, J.M. and Gryna, F.M., *Quality Planning and Analysis*, 2nd Ed., New York: McGraw-Hill, 1980.

Kanholm, J., *ISO 9000 Documentation*, Los Angeles: AQA Press, 1993.

Kanholm, J., *ISO 9000 Explained*, Los Angeles: AQA Press, 1993.

Kanholm, J., *ISO 9000 in Your Company*, Los Angeles: AQA Press, 1993.

Likert, T., *New Patterns of Management*, New York: McGraw-Hill, 1961.

Livingston, J. S., "Pygmalion in Management," *Harvard Business Review*, Cambridge, MA, July/Aug., 1969.

Maslow, A. H., *Motivation and Personality*, New York: Harper and Row, 1970.

McGregor, D., *The Human Side of Enterprise*, New York: McGraw-Hill, 1960.

Montgomery, D. C., *Design and Analysis of Experiments*, 3rd Ed., New York: Wiley, 1991.

Montgomery, D. C., *Introduction to Statistical Quality Control*, New York: Wiley, 1985.

Ott, E. R., *Process Quality Control*, New York: McGraw-Hill, 1975.

Perez-Wilson, M., *Machine/Process Capability Study*, Scottsdale, AZ: Advanced Systems Consultants, 1989.

Peters, T. J. and Waterman, R. A., *In Search of Excellence*, New York: Harper and Row, 1982.

Peters, T. J., *Thriving on Chaos*, New York: Harper and Row, 1987.

Pyzdek, T., *Pyzdek's Guide to SPC, Volume One: Fundamentals*, Tucson, AZ: Quality Publishing, 1989 (a Quality Press, ASQC, publication).

Pyzdek, T., *An SPC Primer*, Tucson, AZ: Quality Publishing, 1986 (a Quality Press, ASQC, publication).

ReVelle, J. B., *The New Quality Technology*, Los Angeles: Hughes Aircraft, 1988.

Schatz and Schatz, *Managing by Influence*, Englewood Cliffs, NJ: Prentice Hall, 1986.

Scholtes, P. R., *The Team Handbook*, Madison, WI: Joiner Associates, 1988.

Scott and Jaffe, *Empowerment*, Los Altos, CA: Crisp Publications, 1991.

Senge, P. M., *The Fifth Discipline*, New York: Doubleday, 1990.

Sepehri, M., *Quest for Quality*, Norcross, GA: Industrial Engineering and Management Press, IIE, 1987.

Shewhart, W. A., *Economic Control of Quality of Manufactured Product*, New York: D. Van Nostrand, 1931.

Shewhart, W. A., *Statistical Method from the Viewpoint of Quality Control*, Lancaster PA: Lancaster Press, 1939.

Taguchi, G., and Wu, Y., *Taguchi Methods: On-Line Production*, Japanese Standards Association and ASI Press, Allen Park, MI, 1994.

Total Quality Management Guide, Office of the Deputy Assistant Secretary of Defense, OASD (P&L) TQM, Pentagon, Washington, DC, 1989.

Total Quality Management Implementation: Selected Readings, Office of the Assistant Secretary of Defense, (P&L) TQM/IPO, Washington, DC, 1989.

Traver, R. W., *Industrial Problem Solving*, Carol Stream, IL: Hitchcock, 1989.

Watson, *Strategic Benchmarking*, Milwaukee, WI: ASQC Press, 1994.

Whitehouse, G. E., *Systems Analysis and Design Using Network Techniques*, Englewood Cliffs, NJ: Prentice Hall, 1973.

Quality Control Tables For SPC

Table 1 Areas Under the Normal Curve
(Proportion of Total Area Under the Curve From $-\infty$ to Designated Z Value)

Z	0.09	0.08	0.07	0.06	0.05	0.04	0.03	0.02	0.01	0.00
-3.5	0.00017	0.00017	0.00018	0.00019	0.00019	0.00020	0.00021	0.00022	0.00022	0.00023
-3.4	0.00024	0.00025	0.00026	0.00027	0.00028	0.00029	0.00030	0.00031	0.00033	0.00034
-3.3	0.00035	0.00036	0.00038	0.00039	0.00040	0.00042	0.00043	0.00045	0.00047	0.00048
-3.2	0.00050	0.00052	0.00054	0.00056	0.00058	0.00060	0.00062	0.00064	0.00066	0.00069
-3.1	0.00071	0.00074	0.00076	0.00079	0.00082	0.00085	0.00087	0.00090	0.00094	0.00097
-3.0	0.00100	0.00104	0.00107	0.00111	0.00114	0.00118	0.00122	0.00126	0.00131	0.00135
-2.9	0.0014	0.0014	0.0015	0.0015	0.0016	0.0016	0.0017	0.0017	0.0018	0.0019
-2.8	0.0019	0.0020	0.0021	0.0021	0.0022	0.0023	0.0023	0.0024	0.0025	0.0026
-2.7	0.0026	0.0027	0.0028	0.0029	0.0030	0.0031	0.0032	0.0033	0.0034	0.0035
-2.6	0.0036	0.0037	0.0038	0.0039	0.0040	0.0041	0.0043	0.0044	0.0045	0.0047
-2.5	0.0048	0.0049	0.0051	0.0052	0.0054	0.0055	0.0057	0.0059	0.0060	0.0062
-2.4	0.0064	0.0066	0.0068	0.0069	0.0071	0.0073	0.0075	0.0078	0.0080	0.0082
-2.3	0.0084	0.0087	0.0089	0.0091	0.0094	0.0096	0.0099	0.0102	0.0104	0.0107
-2.2	0.0110	0.0113	0.0116	0.0119	0.0122	0.0125	0.0129	0.0132	0.0136	0.0139
-2.1	0.0143	0.0146	0.0150	0.0154	0.0158	0.0162	0.0166	0.0170	0.0174	0.0179
-2.0	0.0183	0.0188	0.0192	0.0197	0.0202	0.0207	0.0212	0.0217	0.0222	0.0228
-1.9	0.0233	0.0239	0.0244	0.0250	0.0256	0.0262	0.0268	0.0274	0.0281	0.0287
-1.8	0.0294	0.0301	0.0307	0.0314	0.0322	0.0329	0.0336	0.0344	0.0351	0.0359
-1.7	0.0367	0.0375	0.0384	0.0392	0.0401	0.0409	0.0418	0.0427	0.0436	0.0446
-1.6	0.0455	0.0465	0.0475	0.0485	0.0495	0.0505	0.0516	0.0526	0.0537	0.0548
-1.5	0.0559	0.0571	0.0582	0.0594	0.0606	0.0618	0.0630	0.0643	0.0655	0.0668
-1.4	0.0681	0.0694	0.0708	0.0721	0.0735	0.0749	0.0764	0.0778	0.0793	0.0808
-1.3	0.0823	0.0838	0.0853	0.0869	0.0885	0.0901	0.0918	0.0934	0.0951	0.0968
-1.2	0.0985	0.1003	0.1020	0.1038	0.1057	0.1075	0.1093	0.1112	0.1131	0.1151
-1.1	0.1170	0.1190	0.1210	0.1230	0.1251	0.1271	0.1292	0.1314	0.1335	0.1357
-1.0	0.1379	0.1401	0.1423	0.1446	0.1469	0.1492	0.1515	0.1539	0.1562	0.1587
-0.9	0.1611	0.1635	0.1660	0.1685	0.1711	0.1736	0.1762	0.1788	0.1814	0.1841
-0.8	0.1867	0.1894	0.1922	0.1949	0.1977	0.2005	0.2033	0.2061	0.2090	0.2119
-0.7	0.2148	0.2177	0.2207	0.2236	0.2266	0.2297	0.2327	0.2358	0.2389	0.2420
-0.6	0.2451	0.2483	0.2514	0.2546	0.2578	0.2611	0.2643	0.2676	0.2709	0.2743
-0.5	0.2776	0.2810	0.2843	0.2877	0.2912	0.2946	0.2981	0.3015	0.3050	0.3085
-0.4	0.3121	0.3156	0.3192	0.3228	0.3264	0.3300	0.3336	0.3372	0.3409	0.3446
-0.3	0.3483	0.3520	0.3557	0.3594	0.3632	0.3669	0.3707	0.3745	0.3783	0.3821
-0.2	0.3859	0.3897	0.3936	0.3974	0.4013	0.4052	0.4090	0.4129	0.4168	0.4207
-0.1	0.4247	0.4286	0.4325	0.4364	0.4404	0.4443	0.4483	0.4522	0.4562	0.4602
-0.0	0.4641	0.4681	0.4721	0.4761	0.4801	0.4840	0.4880	0.4920	0.4960	0.5000

(Continued)

Table 1 Areas Under the Normal Curve *(Continued)*

Z	**0.00**	**0.01**	**0.02**	**0.03**	**0.04**	**0.05**	**0.06**	**0.07**	**0.08**	**0.09**
+0.0	0.5000	0.5040	0.5080	0.5120	0.5160	0.5199	0.5239	0.5279	0.5139	0.5359
+0.1	0.5398	0.5438	0.5478	0.5517	0.5557	0.5596	0.5636	0.5675	0.5714	0.5753
+0.2	0.5793	0.5832	0.5871	0.5910	0.5948	0.5987	0.6026	0.6064	0.6103	0.6141
+0.3	0.6179	0.6217	0.6255	0.6293	0.6331	0.6368	0.6406	0.6443	0.6480	0.6517
+0.4	0.6554	0.6591	0.6628	0.6664	0.6700	0.6736	0.6772	0.6808	0.6844	0.6879
+0.5	0.6915	0.6950	0.6985	0.7019	0.7054	0.7088	0.7123	0.7157	0.7190	0.7224
+0.6	0.7257	0.7291	0.7324	0.7357	0.7389	0.7422	0.7454	0.7486	0.7517	0.7549
+0.7	0.7580	0.7611	0.7642	0.7673	0.7704	0.7734	0.7764	0.7794	0.7823	0.7852
+0.8	0.7881	0.7910	0.7939	0.7967	0.7995	0.8023	0.8051	0.8079	0.8106	0.8133
+0.9	0.8159	0.8186	0.8212	0.8238	0.8264	0.8289	0.8315	0.8340	0.8365	0.8389
+1.0	0.8413	0.8438	0.8461	0.8485	0.8508	0.8531	0.8554	0.8577	0.8599	0.8621
+1.1	0.8643	0.8665	0.8686	0.8708	0.8729	0.8749	0.8770	0.8790	0.8810	0.8830
+1.2	0.8849	0.8869	0.8888	0.8907	0.8925	0.8944	0.8962	0.8980	0.8997	0.9015
+1.3	0.9032	0.9049	0.9066	0.9082	0.9099	0.9115	0.9131	0.9147	0.9162	0.9177
+1.4	0.9192	0.9207	0.9222	0.9236	0.9251	0.9265	0.9279	0.9292	0.9306	0.9319
+1.5	0.9332	0.9345	0.9357	0.9370	0.9382	0.9394	0.9406	0.9418	0.9429	0.9441
+1.6	0.9452	0.9463	0.9474	0.9484	0.9495	0.9505	0.9515	0.9525	0.9535	0.9545
+1.7	0.9554	0.9564	0.9573	0.9582	0.9591	0.9599	0.9608	0.9616	0.9625	0.9633
+1.8	0.9641	0.9649	0.9656	0.9664	0.9671	0.9678	0.9686	0.9693	0.9699	0.9706
+1.9	0.9713	0.9719	0.9726	0.9732	0.9738	0.9744	0.9750	0.9756	0.9761	0.9767
+2.0	0.9773	0.9778	0.9783	0.9788	0.9793	0.9798	0.9803	0.9808	0.9812	0.9817
+2.1	0.9821	0.9826	0.9830	0.9834	0.9838	0.9842	0.9846	0.9850	0.9854	0.9857
+2.2	0.9861	0.9864	0.9868	0.9871	0.9875	0.9878	0.9881	0.9884	0.9887	0.9890
+2.3	0.9893	0.9896	0.9898	0.9901	0.9904	0.9906	0.9909	0.9911	0.9913	0.9916
+2.4	0.9918	0.9920	0.9922	0.9925	0.9927	0.9929	0.9931	0.9932	0.9934	0.9936
+2.5	0.9938	0.9940	0.9941	0.9943	0.9945	0.9946	0.9948	0.9949	0.9951	0.9952
+2.6	0.9953	0.9955	0.9956	0.9957	0.9959	0.9960	0.9961	0.9962	0.9963	0.9964
+2.7	0.9965	0.9966	0.9967	0.9968	0.9969	0.9970	0.9971	039972	0.9973	0.9974
+2.8	0.9974	0.9975	0.9976	0.9977	0.9977	0.9978	0.9979	0.9979	0.9980	0.9981
+2.9	0.9981	0.9982	0.9983	0.9983	0.9984	0.9984	0.9985	0.9985	0.9986	0.9986
+3.0	0.99865	0.99869	0.99874	0.99878	0.99882	0.99886	0.99889	0.99893	0.99896	0.99900
+3.1	0.99903	0.99906	0.99910	0.99913	0.99915	0.99918	0.99921	0.99924	0.99926	0.99929
+3.2	0.99931	0.99934	0.99936	0.99938	0.99940	0.99942	0.99944	0.99946	0.99948	0.99950
+3.3	0.99952	0.99953	0.99955	0.99957	0.99958	0.99960	0.99961	0.99962	0.99964	0.99965
+3.4	0.99966	0.99967	0.99969	0.99970	0.99971	0.99972	0.99973	0.99974	0.99975	0.99976
+3.5	0.99977	0.99978	0.99978	0.99979	0.99980	0.99981	0.99981	0.99982	0.99983	0.99983

$z = (x_i - \mu)/\sigma$

$P_S = P(z \leq z_i)$

$P_Z = P(z \leq z_i)$

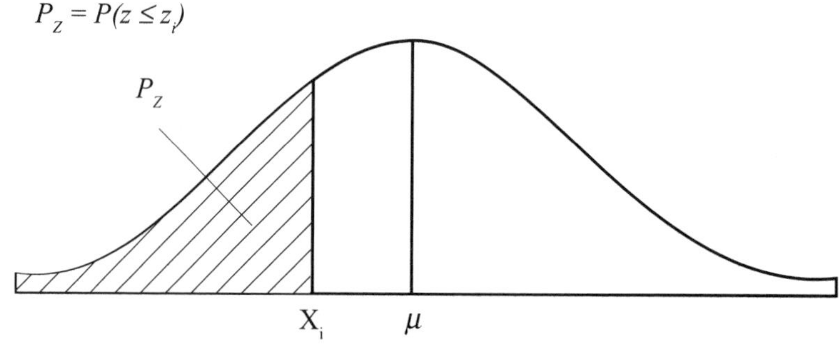

Table 2 Factors for Computing 3σ Control Chart Limits

Subsample Size	A_2	A_3	B3	B_4	D_3	D_4
2	1.880	2.659	0.000	3.267	0.000	3.267
3	1.023	1.954	0.000	2.568	0.000	2.575
4	0.729	1.628	0.000	2.266	0.000	2.282
5	0.577	1.427	0.000	2.089	0.000	2.115
6	0.483	1.287	0.030	1.970	0.000	2.004
7	0.419	1.182	0.118	1.882	0.076	1.924
8	0.373	1.099	0.185	1.815	0.136	1.864
9	0.337	1.032	0.239	1.761	0.184	1.816
10	0.308	0.975	0.284	1.716	0.223	1.777
11	0.285	0.927	0.321	1.679	0.256	1.774
12	0.266	0.886	0.354	1.646	0.284	1.716
13	0.249	0.850	0.382	1.618	0.308	1.692
14	0.235	0.817	0.406	1.594	0.329	1.671
15	0.223	0.789	0.428	1.572	0.348	1.652

Subsample Size	d_2	D_1	D_2
2	1.128	0.000	3.686
3	1.693	0.000	4.358
4	2.059	0.000	4.698
5	2.326	0.000	4.918
6	2.534	0.000	5.078
7	2.704	0.205	5.203
8	2.847	0.387	5.307
9	2.970	0.546	5.394
10	3.078	0.687	5.469
11	3.173	0.812	5.534
12	3.258	0.924	5.592
13	3.336	1.026	5.646
14	3.407	1.121	5.693
15	3.472	1.207	5.737

Values for subsample sizes to 25 and above are available (see Montgomery 1985, Appendix VI).

Table 3 Summation of Terms of Poisson's Exponential Binomial Limit
(1,000 x Probability of *c* or less occurrences of event that has average number of occurrences equal to *np* or λT)

d (or) c / np λT	0	1	2	3	4	5	6	7	8	9
0.02	980	1000								
0.04	961	999	1000							
0.06	942	998	1000							
0.08	923	997	1000							
0.10	905	995	1000							
0.15	861	990	999	1000						
0.20	819	982	999	1000						
0.25	779	974	998	1000						
0.30	741	963	996	1000						
0.35	705	951	994	1000						
0.40	670	938	992	999	1000					
0.45	638	925	989	999	1000					
0.50	607	910	986	998	1000					
0.55	577	894	982	998	1000					
0.60	549	878	977	997	1000					
0.65	522	861	972	996	999	1000				
0.70	497	844	966	994	999	1000				
0.75	472	827	959	993	999	1000				
0.80	449	809	953	991	999	1000				
0.85	427	791	945	989	998	1000				
0.90	407	772	937	987	998	1000				
0.95	387	754	929	984	997	1000				
1.00	368	736	920	981	996	999	1000			
1.1	333	699	900	974	995	999	1000			
1.2	301	663	879	966	992	998	1000			
1.3	273	627	857	957	989	998	1000			
1.4	247	592	833	946	986	997	999	1000		
1.5	223	558	809	934	981	996	999	1000		
1.6	202	525	783	921	976	994	999	1000		
1.7	183	493	757	907	970	992	998	1000		
1.8	165	463	731	891	964	990	997	999	1000	
1.9	150	434	704	875	956	987	997	999	1000	
2.0	135	406	677	857	947	983	995	999	1000	

(Continued)

Table 3 Summation of Terms of Poisson's Exponential Binomial Limit *(Continued)*

np / λT \ d (or) c	0	1	2	3	4	5	6	7	8	9
2.2	111	355	623	819	928	975	993	998	1000	
2.4	091	308	570	779	904	964	988	997	999	1000
2.6	074	267	518	736	877	951	983	995	999	1000
2.8	061	231	469	692	848	935	976	992	998	999
3.0	050	199	423	647	815	916	966	988	996	999
3.2	041	171	380	603	781	895	955	983	994	998
3.4	033	147	340	558	744	871	942	977	992	997
3.6	027	126	303	515	706	844	927	969	988	996
3.8	022	107	269	473	668	816	909	960	984	994
4.0	018	092	238	433	629	785	889	949	979	992
4.2	015	078	210	395	590	753	867	936	972	989
4.4	012	066	185	359	551	720	844	921	964	985
4.6	010	056	163	326	513	686	818	905	955	980
4.8	008	048	143	294	476	651	791	887	944	975
5.0	007	040	125	265	440	616	762	867	932	968
5.2	006	034	109	238	406	581	732	845	918	960
5.4	005	029	095	213	373	546	702	822	903	951
5.6	004	024	082	191	342	512	670	797	886	941
5.8	003	021	072	170	313	478	638	771	867	929
6.0	002	017	062	151	285	446	606	744	847	916

	10	11	12	13	14	15	16
2.8	1000						
3.0	1000						
3.2	1000						
3.4	999	1000					
3.6	999	1000					
3.8	998	999	1000				
4.0	997	999	1000				
4.2	996	999	1000				
4.4	994	998	999	1000			
4.6	992	997	999	1000			
4.8	990	996	999	1000			
5.0	986	995	998	999	1000		
5.2	982	993	997	999	1000		
5.4	977	990	996	999	1000		
5.6	972	988	995	998	999	1000	
5.8	965	984	993	997	999	1000	
6.0	957	980	991	996	999	999	1000

(Continued)

Table 3 Summation of Terms of Poisson's Exponential Binomial Limit *(Continued)*

np / λT \ d (or) c	0	1	2	3	4	5	6	7	8	9
6.2	002	015	054	134	259	414	574	716	826	902
6.4	002	012	046	119	235	384	542	687	803	886
6.6	001	010	040	105	213	355	511	658	780	869
6.8	001	009	034	093	192	327	480	628	755	850
7.0	001	007	030	082	173	301	450	599	729	830
7.2	001	006	025	072	156	276	420	569	703	810
7.4	001	005	022	063	140	253	392	539	676	788
7.6	001	004	019	055	125	231	365	510	648	765
7.8	000	004	016	048	112	210	338	481	620	741
8.0	000	003	014	042	100	191	313	453	593	717
8.5	000	002	009	030	074	150	256	386	523	653
9.0	000	001	006	021	055	116	207	324	456	587
9.5	000	001	004	015	040	089	165	269	392	522
10.0	000	000	003	010	029	067	130	220	333	458
	10	11	12	13	14	15	16	17	18	19
6.2	949	975	989	995	998	999	1000			
6.4	939	969	986	994	997	999	1000			
6.6	927	963	982	992	997	999	999	1000		
6.8	915	955	978	990	996	998	999	1000		
7.0	901	947	973	987	994	998	999	1000		
7.2	887	937	967	984	993	997	999	999	1000	
7.4	871	926	961	980	991	996	998	999	1000	
7.6	854	915	954	976	989	995	998	999	1000	
7.8	835	902	945	971	986	993	997	999	1000	
8.0	816	888	936	966	983	992	996	998	999	1000
8.5	763	849	909	949	973	986	993	997	999	999
9.0	706	803	876	926	959	978	989	995	998	999
9.5	645	752	836	898	940	967	982	991	996	998
10.0	583	697	792	864	917	951	973	986	993	997
	20	21	22							
8.5	1000									
9.0	1000									
9.5	999	1000								
10.0	998	999	1000							

(Continued)

Table 3 Summation of Terms of Poisson's Exponential Binomial Limit *(Continued)*

d (or) c / np λT	0	1	2	3	4	5	6	7	8	9
10.5	000	000	002	007	021	050	102	179	279	397
11.0	000	000	001	005	015	038	079	143	232	341
11.5	000	000	001	003	011	028	060	114	191	289
12.0	000	000	001	002	008	020	046	090	155	242
12.5	000	000	000	002	005	015	035	070	125	201
13.0	000	000	000	001	004	011	026	054	100	166
13.5	000	000	000	001	003	008	019	041	079	135
14.0	000	000	000	000	002	006	014	032	062	109
14.5	000	000	000	000	001	004	010	124	048	088
15.0	000	000	000	000	001	003	008	018	037	070
	10	11	12	13	14	15	16	17	18	19
10.5	521	639	742	825	888	932	960	978	988	994
11.0	460	579	689	781	854	907	944	968	982	991
11.5	402	520	633	733	815	878	924	954	974	986
12.0	347	462	576	682	772	844	899	937	963	979
12.5	297	406	519	628	725	806	869	916	948	969
13.0	252	353	463	573	675	764	835	890	930	957
13.5	211	304	409	518	623	718	798	861	908	942
14.0	176	260	358	464	570	669	756	827	883	923
14.5	145	220	311	413	518	619	711	790	853	901
15.0	118	185	268	363	466	568	664	749	819	875
	20	21	22	23	24	25	26	27	28	29
10.5	997	999	999	1000						
11.0	995	998	999	1000						
11.5	992	996	998	999	1000					
12.0	988	994	997	999	999	1000				
12.5	983	991	995	998	999	999	1000			
13.0	975	986	992	996	998	999	1000			
13.5	965	980	989	994	997	998	999	1000		
14.0	952	971	983	991	995	997	999	999	1000	
14.5	936	960	976	986	992	996	998	999	999	1000
15.0	917	947	967	981	989	994	997	998	999	1000

(Continued)

Table 3 Summation of Terms of Poisson's Exponential Binomial Limit *(Continued)*

np / λT \ d (or) c	4	5	6	7	8	9	10	11	12	13
16	000	001	004	010	022	043	077	127	193	275
17	000	001	002	005	013	026	049	085	135	201
18	000	000	001	003	007	015	030	055	092	143
19	000	000	001	002	004	009	018	035	061	098
20	000	000	000	001	002	005	011	021	039	066
21	000	000	000	000	001	003	006	013	025	043
22	000	000	000	000	001	002	004	008	015	028
23	000	000	000	000	000	001	002	004	009	017
24	000	000	000	000	000	000	001	003	005	011
25	000	000	000	000	000	000	001	001	003	006
	14	15	16	17	18	19	20	21	22	23
16	368	467	566	659	742	812	868	911	942	963
17	281	371	468	564	655	736	805	861	905	937
18	208	287	375	469	562	651	731	799	855	899
19	150	215	292	378	469	561	647	725	793	849
20	105	157	221	297	381	470	559	644	721	787
21	072	111	163	227	302	384	471	558	640	716
22	048	077	117	169	232	306	387	472	556	637
23	031	052	082	123	175	238	310	389	472	555
24	020	034	056	087	128	180	243	314	392	473
25	012	022	038	060	092	134	185	247	318	394
	24	25	26	27	28	29	30	31	32	33
16	978	987	993	996	998	999	999	1000		
17	959	975	985	991	995	997	999	999	1000	
18	932	955	972	983	990	994	997	998	999	1000
19	893	927	951	969	980	988	993	996	998	999
20	843	888	922	948	966	978	987	992	995	997
21	782	838	883	917	944	963	976	985	991	994
22	712	777	832	877	913	940	959	973	983	989
23	635	708	772	827	873	908	936	956	971	981
24	554	632	704	768	823	868	904	932	953	969
25	473	553	629	700	763	818	863	900	929	950
	34	35	36	37	38	39	40	41	42	43
19	999	1000								
20	999	999	1000							
21	997	998	999	999	1000					
22	994	996	998	999	999	1000				
23	988	993	996	997	999	999	1000			
24	979	987	992	995	997	998	999	999	1000	
25	966	978	985	991	994	997	998	999	999	1000

— Index —